# A creative idea can grow into a series.

SCHOLASTIC

LITERACY PLACE®

Copyright acknowledgments and credits appear on page 136, which constitutes an extension of this copyright page.

Copyright © 1996 by Scholastic Inc.          All rights reserved.          Printed in the U.S.A.
                                             ISBN 0-590-49109-1
            5 6 7 8 9 10                          24          02 01 00 99 98 97

# Visit a
# Publishing Company

**A creative idea can grow into a series.**

# What a Character!

## Hit series often have memorable characters.

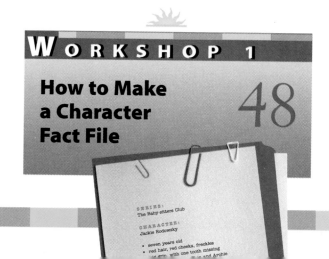

SERIES:
The Baby-sitters Club

CHARACTER:
Jackie Rodowsky

• seven years old
• red hair, red cheeks, freckles
• red hair, with one tooth missing
• and Archie

# A Series for Everyone

## There are many different kinds of series.

ANTWON BUTLER
age 8

LITTLE HOUSE IN THE BIG WOODS

# Long-Running Hits

**Some series last for years and years.**

# Trade Books

The following
books accompany this
*Hit Series*
SourceBook.

## Realistic Fiction

### Go Fish

by Mary Stolz
illustrated by
Pat Cummings

## Social Studies Nonfiction

### ...If You Lived at the Time of the Great San Francisco Earthquake

by Ellen Levine
illustrated by
Pat Grant Porter

## Informational Fiction

### Scholastic's The Magic School Bus® Inside the Human Body

by Joanna Cole
illustrated by
Bruce Degen

## Newbery Honor
## Classic Fiction

### Ramona Quimby, Age 8

by Beverly
Cleary
illustrated by
Alan Tiegreen

**Hit series often have memorable characters.**

# What a Character!

Travel along a time line and meet some of your favorite characters. Then board The Magic School Bus with the unforgettable Ms. Frizzle.

Discover how author Joanna Cole and illustrator Bruce Degen create their popular Magic School Bus series.

Join Jessi on a baby-sitting job that fizzles instead of sizzles.

# WORKSHOP 1

Use your imagination to create a new character for your favorite series.

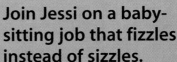

SERIES:
The Baby-sitters Club

CHARACTER:
Jackie Rodowsky

- seven years old
- red hair, red cheeks, freckles
- with one tooth missing

# A CENTURY of Hits

They're in books, in movies, on TV, and on your computer screen. They're almost everywhere you look. Who are they? Your favorite characters!

## 1900　1910　1920

### 1902

### Peter Rabbit

*The Tale of Peter Rabbit* hopped to fame as the best-selling children's book ever.

### 1924

### The Boxcar Children

All aboard! The author longed to live in a caboose. She couldn't, but she created characters who did.

## Batman

Batman didn't start out with his trademark cape and costume. At first, the artist drew him with stiff bat's wings and a red outfit!

**1939**

## Lassie

A dog named Pal was the first Lassie. The latest Lassie is Pal's great-great-great-great-great-grandson.

**1943**

**1950**

## Ramona

The world's most famous pest lives on Klickitat Street, a real street in Portland, Oregon. The author grew up just a few blocks away.

## Madeline

There are actually two Madelines. One is the French school girl. The other is . . . the author's wife!

# 1930    1940    1950

**1931**

## Babar

Babar began in France as a bedtime story. The well-dressed elephant now stars worldwide in books, on TV, and on cassette.

**1950**

## Charlie Brown

The *Apollo 10* astronauts named their command ship *Charlie Brown*. Naturally, they called the lunar module . . . *Snoopy!*

## 1969
### Kermit
Kermit started out being a lizard! He was changed into a frog just before he made his bow on *Sesame Street*.

## 1963
### Encyclopedia Brown
The boy detective speaks only English. But his adventures have been translated into 14 different languages!

## 1962
### Clifford
Talk about big! This red dog isn't just a book and video. He's a giant balloon in New York's Thanksgiving Day Parade.

# 1960      1970

## 1963
### Amelia Bedelia
Who but Amelia Bedelia would put sponges in sponge cake? The author, that's who! She tried out *all* of Amelia's recipes.

## 1971
### Chapulin Colorado
The "red grasshopper" leaped over the border from Mexico. Now he struts his stuff on Spanish-language TV channels here.

## Carmen Sandiego

Where is Carmen Sandiego? Millions of players track her across their computer screens. They chase her on TV, too!

**1988**

## Iktomi

Iktomi is a trickster in the folklore of the Lakota people. He's so tricky that he goes by at least 10 different names!

**1981**

## Julian

Where do stories come from? Author Ann Cameron got some of hers from the true adventures of her friend, Julian DeWetts.

**1985**

# 1980                    1990····▶

**1986**

## The Baby-sitters Club

Call these baby-sitters and what do you get? The country's most popular middle-grade series.

**1986**

## Ms. Frizzle

The Friz drove the Magic School Bus right off the page and onto your television screen.

**1991**

## The Time Warp Trio

These three have the time of their lives as they warp from the Stone Age to the Old West and back. Who knows where they'll be going next!

Scholastic's

from

## Scholastic's The Magic School Bus Hops Home

**a TV Script** by Jocelyn Stevenson

illustrated by **Nancy Stevenson**

based on **The Magic School Bus**® book series

by **JOANNA COLE** and **BRUCE DEGEN**

# FROM THE DESK OF MS. FRIZZLE

Time for another adventure on The Magic School Bus!

This week, we're studying habitats—the places where animals live. Wanda wanted to do her part, so she brought her bullfrog Bella to school. Wanda tried to make a perfect classroom habitat for Bella, but Bella had other ideas. When Arnold opened a window, Bella hopped out!

Ms. Frizzle

Wanda

Dorothy Ann

Keesha

Phoebe

Arnold

Tim

Ralphie

Carlos

Liz the Lizard

# THE MAGIC SCHOOL BUS
# HOPS HOME

## CHARACTERS

| | |
|---|---|
| WANDA | PHOEBE |
| ARNOLD | KEESHA |
| RALPHIE | CARLOS |
| TIM | DOROTHY ANN |
| MS. FRIZZLE | LIZ THE LIZARD |

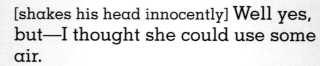

[INTERIOR OF MS. FRIZZLE'S CLASSROOM. DAYTIME.]

### WANDA

Arnold!! Bella's gone!!!

### ARNOLD

Gone? Where?

### WANDA

Out the window! Arnold, did you open it?

### ARNOLD

[shakes his head innocently] Well yes, but—I thought she could use some air.

[Everyone runs to the window to look out. RALPHIE comes up to ARNOLD.]

### RALPHIE

Nice one, Arnold.

[WANDA wanders grief–stricken around the room.]

### WANDA

Why would Bella leave? Why? Why? Why? It's so perfect here!

[TIM holds up the duck mug in one hand and the beanbag frog in the other.]

### TIM

Maybe she needed more from her habitat than a duck mug and a beanbag shaped like a frog …

[WANDA takes the mug and beanbag away from TIM and puts them with all of Bella's other toys.]

### WANDA

Tim, those were her special things!

[WANDA faces everyone.]

### WANDA

I've got to find her!

[Then she grabs ARNOLD, who's trying to sneak back to his desk.]

### WANDA

And you've got to help me.

[She grabs the beanbag frog.]

### WANDA

Ms. Frizzle? Could we be excused to go look for Bella?

[MS. FRIZZLE raises an eyebrow at LIZ, who starts to pack up her hammock.]

### MS. FRIZZLE

That's an excellent idea, Wanda! In fact …

17

CUT TO means to quickly change from one scene to another.

[MS. FRIZZLE'S dragonfly earrings start to spin.]

### MS. FRIZZLE

... why don't we make it a ...

[The kids run for the door.]

### ARNOLD

Oh no!

### KIDS

Field trip!!!

[CUT TO: INTERIOR OF MAGIC SCHOOL BUS. DAYTIME. MS. FRIZZLE is at the wheel. WANDA sits right behind her, clutching her beanbag frog, worrying. LIZ is stringing up her hammock. ARNOLD climbs on the bus and takes a seat.]

### ARNOLD

I think I should have stayed home today.

### WANDA

I think Bella should have stayed home today! How are we ever going to find her? She could have hopped anywhere!

### MS. FRIZZLE

Not exactly anywhere, Wanda. As I always say, to find a frog, be a frog.

[MS. FRIZZLE starts pushing buttons on the dashboard.]

### ARNOLD

Be a frog?!! Oh no! Does that
mean we're going to …

[CUT TO: EXTERIOR OF MAGIC SCHOOL BUS.
Through some funny changes, it shrinks to the size of a
very large bullfrog—complete with frogs' legs. Now it is
a bus/frog.]

### ARNOLD

… shrink …

[The BUS/FROG hops past an amazed cat, toward rear of
school, and out of frame.]

### KIDS

[OFF] Whoooaaaaaaaaahhhhhh!!!

[CUT TO: INTERIOR OF BUS/FROG.
The kids look as if they're riding a bucking bronco,
and RALPHIE doesn't like it.]

### RALPHIE

Hey, take it easy.

[LIZ is hanging onto her hammock for dear life. WANDA
and ARNOLD peer anxiously out the window, as the
landscape rises and falls with each hop. MS. FRIZZLE
sings to herself, happy as a clam.]

### MS. FRIZZLE

[humming] "Where oh where has
my little frog gone. …"

[WANDA leans forward—suddenly excited!]

### WANDA

Ms. Frizzle, maybe Bella just
hopped out to find some food!

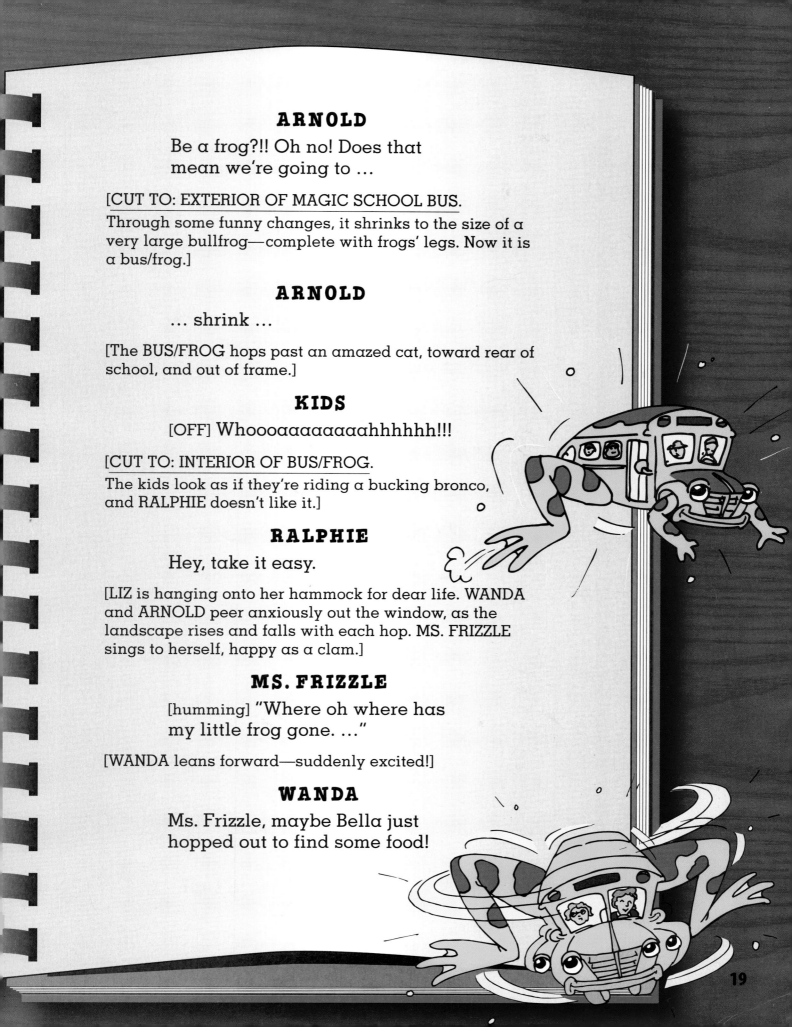

SHOT OF means a picture taken by the camera.

[SHOT OF RALPHIE who dizzily watches the landscape go by.]

### RALPHIE

Food? Who can think of food at a time like this?

[SHOT OF MS. FRIZZLE, who smiles.]

### MS. FRIZZLE

That is definitely a speculation worth consideration, Wanda!

### ARNOLD

What kind of food? Cornflakes? Malloblasters?

### WANDA

Bugs!

### PHOEBE

[gasps] Eeww!!

[SHOT OF KEESHA, who's enjoying this.]

### KEESHA

Maybe we should hop to the nearest bug habitat to have a look!

### MS. FRIZZLE

What do you say, class?

[SHOT OF RALPHIE clutching his stomach.]

### RALPHIE

Uh, Ms. Frizzle, do we have to hop?

[EXTERIOR. CLEARING.

We see a clearing complete with birds, a dead log, a few trees, and low growing plants and bushes. BUS/FROG hops into frame, landing beside log. BUS/FROG stops and the door opens.]

### MS. FRIZZLE

Everybody out!

[SHOT OF the kids who slowly climb out of BUS/FROG and look around. LIZ stumbles out, dragging her hammock behind her. WANDA pushes past.]

### WANDA

[calling] Bella! Bella! Where are you?? Belllaaaaahhhh!!!

[ARNOLD cringes from the volume of her voice.]

### ARNOLD

Wanda! Quiet! You'll scare her away!

### WANDA

[frustrated] Thanks to you, she's already away, Arnold. The question is where!

[Before another argument can start, a very big grasshopper hops by. MS. FRIZZLE scoops LIZ (with hammock) up into her arms and hops onto the grasshopper's back.]

### MS. FRIZZLE

Hop along, class! Two by two, please!!

[Kids hop after MS. FRIZZLE, all except for RALPHIE, who's still feeling a little ill.]

A WIDE SHOT is a picture that shows a wide area.

### RALPHIE

Thanks, but I'll wa-a-alk!!!

[A beetle scuttles between RALPHIE'S legs, taking him with it.]

### RALPHIE

Whoa!!

[WIDE SHOT. Top of the log. MS. FRIZZLE and LIZ get off their grasshopper. The kids scramble up after her, dodging bugs. The place is crawling with them!]

### CARLOS

Hey, this place is crawling with frog food!

[RALPHIE gets dumped by his beetle.]

### RALPHIE

Oooff! [moans] Do you have to keep talking about food?

[MS. FRIZZLE helps him up.]

### MS. FRIZZLE

Sorry, Ralphie, but food is one of the things all plants and animals need from their habitat.

[WANDA bears down on ARNOLD.]

### WANDA

So, here's the food, Arnold. Where's Bella?

[ARNOLD lifts up leaves, fungi, moss looking for BELLA.]

### ARNOLD

I'm looking … I'm looking.

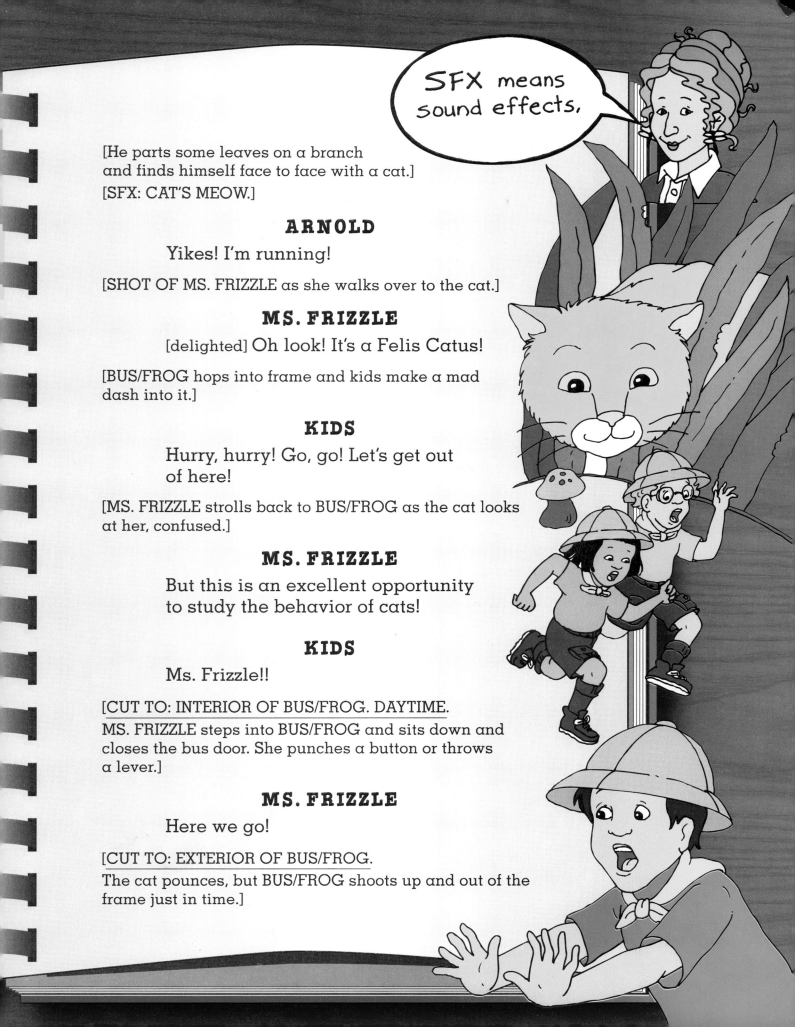

SFX means sound effects.

[He parts some leaves on a branch and finds himself face to face with a cat.]
[SFX: CAT'S MEOW.]

### ARNOLD

Yikes! I'm running!

[SHOT OF MS. FRIZZLE as she walks over to the cat.]

### MS. FRIZZLE

[delighted] Oh look! It's a Felis Catus!

[BUS/FROG hops into frame and kids make a mad dash into it.]

### KIDS

Hurry, hurry! Go, go! Let's get out of here!

[MS. FRIZZLE strolls back to BUS/FROG as the cat looks at her, confused.]

### MS. FRIZZLE

But this is an excellent opportunity to study the behavior of cats!

### KIDS

Ms. Frizzle!!

[CUT TO: INTERIOR OF BUS/FROG. DAYTIME.
MS. FRIZZLE steps into BUS/FROG and sits down and closes the bus door. She punches a button or throws a lever.]

### MS. FRIZZLE

Here we go!

[CUT TO: EXTERIOR OF BUS/FROG.
The cat pounces, but BUS/FROG shoots up and out of the frame just in time.]

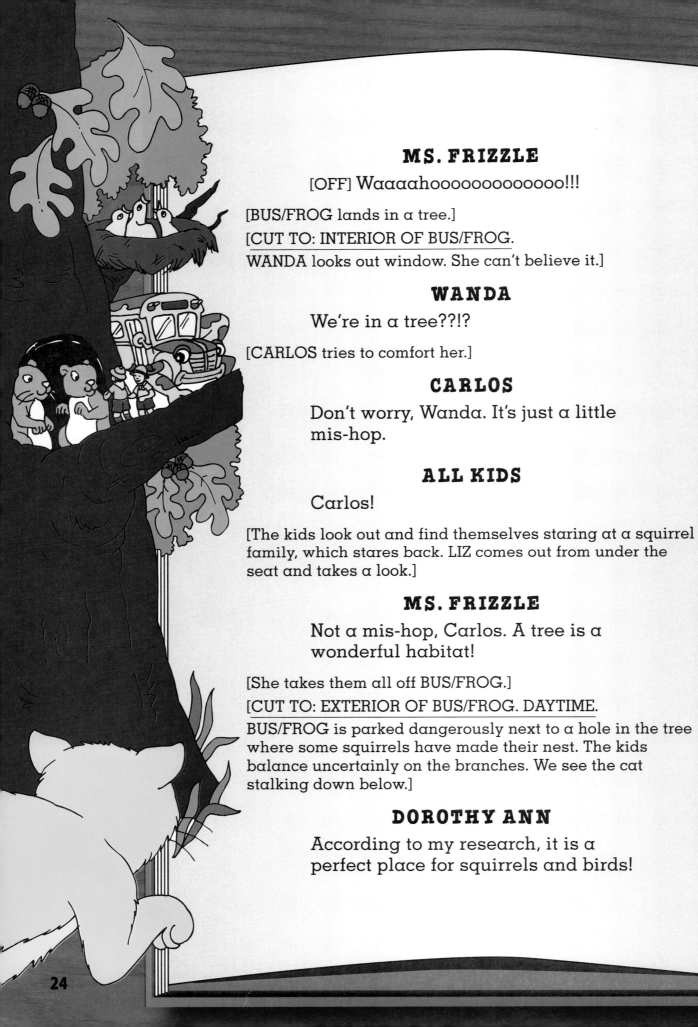

### MS. FRIZZLE

[OFF] Waaaahooooooooooooo!!!

[BUS/FROG lands in a tree.]
[CUT TO: INTERIOR OF BUS/FROG.
WANDA looks out window. She can't believe it.]

### WANDA

We're in a tree??!?

[CARLOS tries to comfort her.]

### CARLOS

Don't worry, Wanda. It's just a little mis-hop.

### ALL KIDS

Carlos!

[The kids look out and find themselves staring at a squirrel family, which stares back. LIZ comes out from under the seat and takes a look.]

### MS. FRIZZLE

Not a mis-hop, Carlos. A tree is a wonderful habitat!

[She takes them all off BUS/FROG.]
[CUT TO: EXTERIOR OF BUS/FROG. DAYTIME.
BUS/FROG is parked dangerously next to a hole in the tree where some squirrels have made their nest. The kids balance uncertainly on the branches. We see the cat stalking down below.]

### DOROTHY ANN

According to my research, it is a perfect place for squirrels and birds!

[Bird tweets and flies by. Squirrels scamper down the trees.]

### KEESHA

[looking down at cat] Yeah, it gives them a safe place away from cats to build their nests.

[One of the squirrels moves to reveal baby squirrels.]

### PHOEBE

Oh look! Baby squirrels!

[WANDA is bursting with frustration.]

### WANDA

But I don't want baby squirrels! I want Bella. And there's not enough space for her here. There's no food. Besides, where would she put her swimming pool?

[RALPHIE points to a limb of the tree.]

### RALPHIE

I don't know. How about over there?

### WANDA

Very funny, Ralphie.

[She looks up. Grabbing ARNOLD, she starts to climb.]

### WANDA

Come on, Arnold. Let's see if we can see her.

### ARNOLD

[hesitating] But Wanda …

[SFX: CREAKING BRANCH.]
[WANDA suddenly sees something below hopping away.
Is it a frog?]

### WANDA

There she is! Look! Bella!
Bellllaaahh!

[She pulls ARNOLD after her.]

### ARNOLD

No wait—Wanda!

### WANDA

Bella!

### ARNOLD

Wanda, wait! Be careful! Wanda!

[WANDA falls off the branch, pulling ARNOLD with her.
At the last second, he grabs onto a twig, stopping them
from falling. They hang there. ARNOLD dangles from the
twig and WANDA holds onto ARNOLD'S foot.]

### ARNOLD

What do we do now, Wanda?

[They look down— see cat looking up hungrily—look at
each other . . .]

### WANDA AND ARNOLD

Heeeeellllppp!!!

[SFX: CREAKING BRANCH AS A CREATURE JUMPS OFF.]

[WIDEN to include the hopping creature that caught CAT's eye. It lands in front of CAT down below. It's a praying mantis.]

### ARNOLD

[through clenched teeth] That wasn't Bella, Wanda!

### WANDA

So? I knew that!

### ARNOLD

Then WHY ARE WE HERE??!?

[SFX: BEEP! BEEP! OF BUS/FROG.]

[SHOT OF BUS/FROG hopping onto a branch below ARNOLD and WANDA. Its roof opens and a large funnel emerges. A cheerful and relaxed MS. FRIZZLE is at the wheel and calls through a bullhorn.]

### MS. FRIZZLE

Wanda? Arnold? Come along now! I can't have you two hanging out here all day!

[ARNOLD and WANDA let go and BUS/FROG catches them. BUS/FROG closes its "eyes," leaps off the branch, lands on the ground, and hops away.]

### RALPHIE

Here we go again!

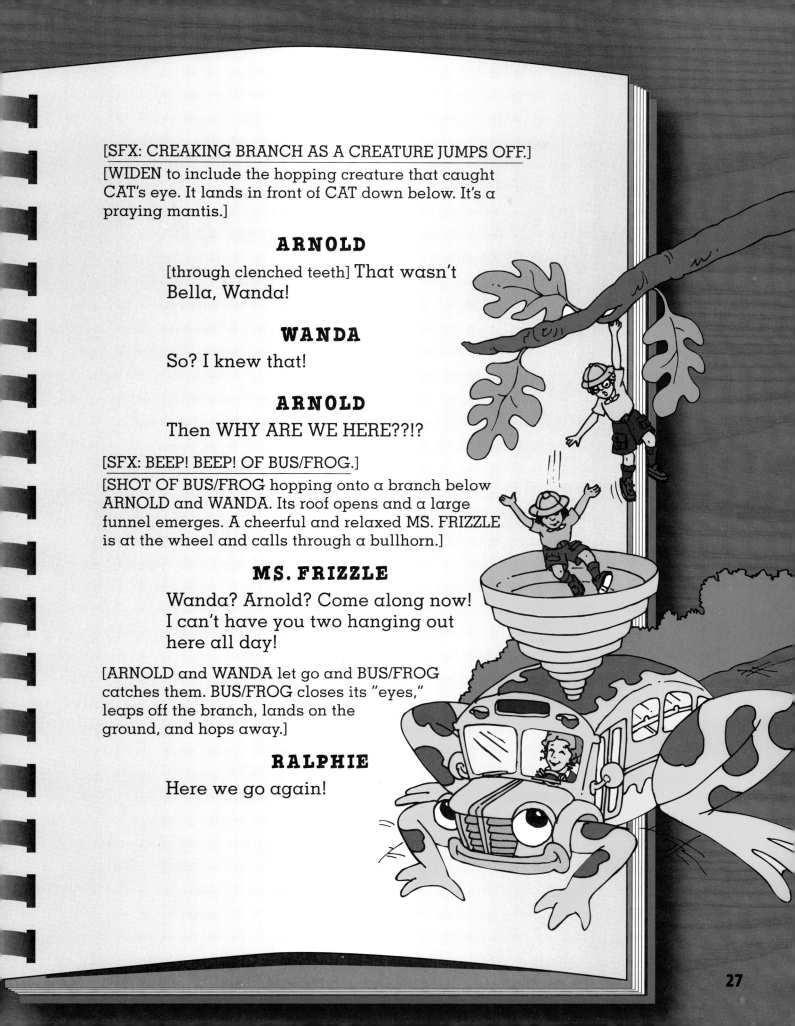

## FROM THE DESK OF MS. FRIZZLE

We followed Bella's trail to a quiet pond and found her sitting on a lily pad. Wanda realized that the pond was a perfect home for Bella, so she tearfully said goodbye. Back in our classroom, Wanda had a real case of the bullfrog blues. But Wanda's sad tale has a "hoppy" ending. We made Wanda a giant paper frog to cheer her up. And that frog's habitat is the classroom.

## THE END

# THE VOICES BEHIND THE SCENES

## MALCOLM-JAMAL WARNER

If the Producer, who often appears at the end of each episode, sounds familiar, it's no wonder! You're hearing the voice of **Malcolm-Jamal Warner.** The actor played Theo on the popular TV comedy, *The Cosby Show*.

## LILY TOMLIN

Actress **Lily Tomlin** was perfect for the voice of Ms. Frizzle. After experimenting with many different voices, Tomlin found one that seemed just right—chirpy and cheerful! She won an Emmy for her portrayal.

## LITTLE RICHARD

Famous rock 'n' roll star **Little Richard** sings *The Magic School Bus* theme song. His hits include a rock 'n' roll version of "Itsy Bitsy Spider."

## LISA YAMANAKA

The voice of Wanda is recorded by **Lisa Yamanaka**. She can also be heard in two other animated TV series, *Little Rosey* and *Family Dog*.

# Joanna Cole & Bruce Degen

## Author and Illustrator

**Creating *books is more fun than* riding a roller coaster!**

**W**ho really drives the Magic School Bus? Did you say Ms. Frizzle? Well, think again. The brains behind the wheel are Joanna Cole and Bruce Degen. Together they create this exciting series.

## PROFILE

**Names:** Joanna Cole, Bruce Degen

**Job:**
*Cole:* author
*Degen:* illustrator

**Former jobs:**
*Cole:* baby-sitter, TV factory worker, editor
*Degen:* opera-scenery painter, art teacher

**Favorite school subjects:**
*Cole:* science
*Degen:* art and reading

**First published books:**
*Cole: Cockroaches*
*Degen: Aunt Possum and the Pumpkin Man*

**Where you'd like to go on the Magic School Bus:**
*Cole*: inside the human body
*Degen:* the South Seas

# QUESTIONS
### for Joanna Cole and Bruce Degen, Author and Illustrator

Here's how *author* **Joanna Cole** and *illustrator* **Bruce Degen** create a *hit series.*

**Q** **How did The Magic School Bus books come about?**

**A** *Cole:* I had been writing children's science books for about 15 years when I began the Magic School Bus series. The idea was a teacher who loves science would take her class on trips where no kids had ever gone before.

**Q** **How do you decide what to write about?**

**A** *Degen:* We brainstorm together. Once, on a cross-country plane trip, we came up with a list of 40 possible topics for our books!

**Q** **What's it like working together on a series?**

**A** *Cole:* Bruce and I make a good team! I research and write the book.
*Degen:* Then I come up with illustrations that go with the text. We have many meetings to figure out exactly what words and pictures go on every page.

**Q** Was Ms. Frizzle inspired by a real person?

**A** *Cole:* Oh, yes. I had a science teacher who was just like Ms. Frizzle—she was so enthusiastic about science! Ms. Frizzle is also a lot like me. I like to explain science to kids.

**Q** How did you decide what to make Ms. Frizzle look like?

**A** *Degen:* I pictured my high school teachers, who often wore simple dresses. To make Ms. Frizzle look distinctive, I added outrageous patterns.

**Q** What about Arnold?

**A** *Cole:* Arnold likes to stay at home—he's the opposite of Ms. Frizzle!

**Q** What's the best thing about working on this series?

**A** *Degen:* It's exciting! *Cole:* We're always learning something new.

**Joanna Cole and Bruce Degen's
Tips to Young Writers**

1 Think of an interesting topic or story. Research it.

2 Plan what you're going to write. Make sketches.

3 Put the text and art together to make a book.

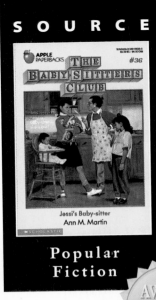

*from*

# THE BABY·SITTERS CLUB

Jessi's Baby-sitter

*by* Ann M. Martin

*illustrated by* Scott Ernster

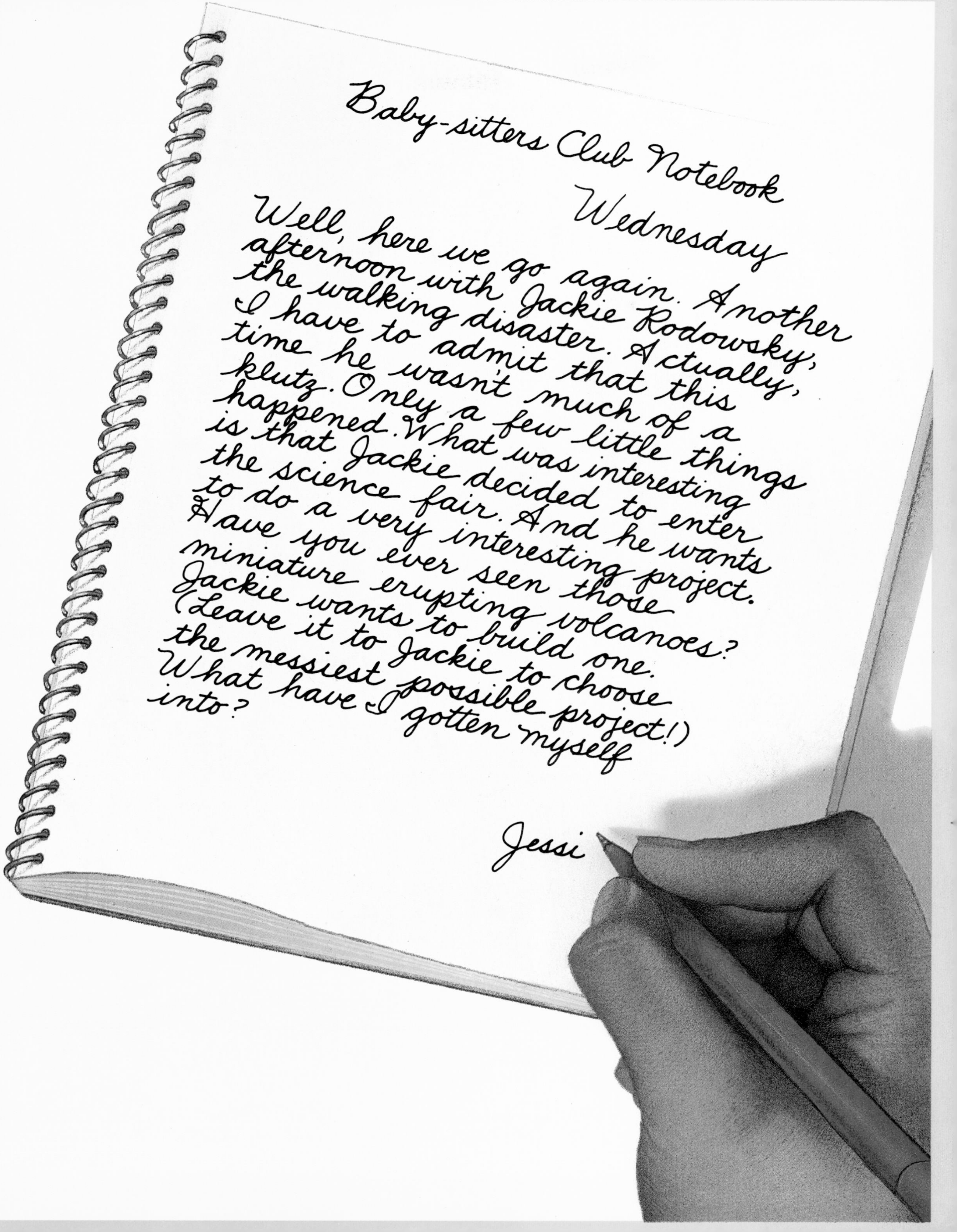

*Baby-sitters Club Notebook*

*Wednesday*

Well, here we go again. Another afternoon with Jackie Rodowsky, the walking disaster. Actually, I have to admit that this time he wasn't much of a klutz. Only a few little things happened. What was interesting is that Jackie decided to enter the science fair. And he wants to do a very interesting project. Have you ever seen those miniature erupting volcanoes? Jackie wants to build one. (Leave it to Jackie to choose the messiest possible project!) What have I gotten myself into?

Jessi

**I**t was the evening of the science fair. I was so excited, you'd think *I'd* entered a project in it. (Well, in a way I had.) Anyway, the kids who were entering had to arrive at Stoneybrook Elementary by six-thirty in order to set up. The fair itself began at seven-thirty.

So at six-thirty, there were Stacey and Charlotte, Mal and Margo, Kristy and David Michael, Jackie and me, and a whole lot of kids and their parents or brothers or sisters or grandparents. Actually, Jackie and I had arrived at 6:20 to make sure we got our table staked out.

Now, at nearly seven o'clock, the all-purpose room was noisy and busy. All around Jackie and me were sighs of relief (when things went right) and groans (when things went wrong). Kids walked by carrying everything from huge pumpkins to complicated electrical things. I could hear the sounds of gears turning, tools tinkering, and video equipment. The all-purpose room was a pretty exciting place to be in.

"How do you feel, Jackie?" I asked him.

His volcano was loaded up and ready to explode. The "Welcome to the World of Volcanic Activity" sign was hung. His pointer was in his hand.

"Fine," he replied, but he sounded nervous. "Listen to this: Igneous rocks are born from fire, the molting—"

"Molten," I corrected him.

"The molten rock that lies several feet—"

"Miles."

"Okay. Several miles below the surface of our wonderful earth."

"Just *our earth*, Jackie. Don't overdo it."

Jackie nodded miserably.

Seven-thirty. The all-purpose room had really filled up. Teachers and parents and families and friends were pouring in.

"Look!" cried Jackie. "There are Mom and Dad and Archie and Shea!"

Boy, did Jackie seem relieved.

The Rodowskys made a beeline for The World of Volcanic Activity.

"Your project looks great, son," exclaimed Jackie's father.

WELCOME to the WORLD of Volcanic Activity

37

"Yeah, it really does," Shea managed to admit.

"You know what?" I said. "I think I'm going to look around at the other projects before the judging begins. Jackie, you stay here and answer questions—but don't set the volcano off, okay?"

Jackie laughed. "Okay." He was beginning to feel pleased with himself. Even Shea hadn't seen the volcano explode. Jackie couldn't wait for the big moment. He wanted to prove something to Shea who, as his big brother, was always several steps ahead of him.

I walked slowly around the room, looking at the displays and experiments. I saw a model of a human heart made from Play-Doh (I think). I saw a small-scale "dinosaur war." I saw an impressive project about the Ice Age. I saw Charlotte's plants with her charts and graphs. One plant was considerably more healthy-looking than the other two, which were sort of scraggly.

"Which plant is that?" I asked, pointing to the full, green one.

"Guess," she said.

"The one that listened to classical music."

"Wrong." Charlotte grinned. "It's the Duran Duran plant. I'm not sure why. Maybe they were just really *fresh* seeds."

I laughed, and continued my walk through the exhibits. When I got back to Jackie's display, I found his family preparing to take a look around, so I said I'd stay with Jackie.

The volcano attracted a lot of attention.

"Neat! What's that?" asked a curly-headed boy.

"A volcano," said Jackie proudly. "It can *erupt*. It makes ash and lava go everywhere. It's really messy."

"Can I see?" asked the boy.

Jackie's face fell. "Sorry. I can only make it explode once. I have to wait until the judges are here. You can see it then."

"Okay," said the boy, looking disappointed.

A few seconds later two girls walked by.

"A volcano!" exclaimed one. "Hey, I've always wondered. What *does* make a volcano?"

Jackie was prepared. "Igneous rocks are born from fire…" He said the entire speech without one mistake. I gave him the thumbs-up sign.

The girl frowned. "But *why*," she went on, "do igneous rocks do that? I mean, why does heat make a volcano erupt?"

Jackie was stumped. That wasn't part of his speech. And he couldn't demonstrate the volcano to the girls, either.

Just when I was beginning to feel bad, my own family showed up. Well, Mama and Daddy and Becca did. Squirt was at home with Aunt Cecilia. Becca had come because she wanted to see Charlotte's experiment, and my parents were there because of the volcano they'd been hearing about.

I began to feel better.

At eight o'clock, an announcement came over the PA system.

"Attention, please. May I have your attention? The judging will now begin. All participants in the science fair prepare to demonstrate and explain your projects to the judges. Visitors, please stand at the back of the room during the judging."

"That was our *prin*cipal," Jackie informed me.

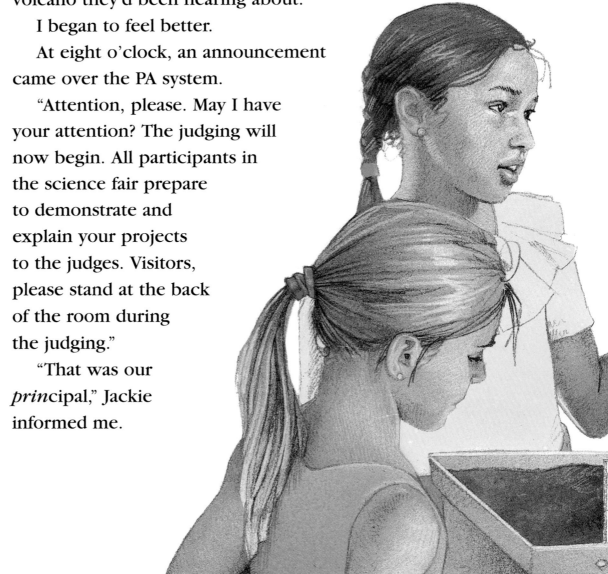

(You'd have thought the President of the United States had just spoken.)

"Good luck, Jackie," I said. "I know you'll do fine. When it's time to make the volcano erupt, tell the judges you have to call me to light the match because you're not allowed to do that yourself."

Jackie swallowed and nodded. I joined my family at the back of the room.

The judging began.

Two women and a man walked solemnly from table to table. They looked each project over. They requested demonstrations. They asked questions.

Welcome to the World of Volcanic Activity

*Asked questions?* Oh, no! Jackie couldn't talk about anything that wasn't in his speech. I hoped fervently that the judges would be so impressed with his demonstration that they wouldn't ask him any questions.

Tick, tick, tick. It was almost eight-thirty.

At last the judges reached The World of Volcanic Activity. I saw Jackie whisper something to one of the women. Then he saw me in the crowd and motioned for me to come forward. I did so, matches in hand.

"This," said Jackie as I reached his table, "is Jessi. She's my helper. She has to light the match for me."

(The judges smiled.)

I lit the match, told everyone to stand back, and tossed the match in the volcano. Jackie threw his hands in the air and cried, "The miracle of a volcano comes to life before our very eyes!"

*PHOO!* Lava was everywhere! It almost spattered the judges. Then it settled into a nice gooey flow down the sides of the volcano. The judges looked extremely impressed.

I stood to the side as Jackie made his speech, using the pointer.

The judges nodded and smiled. And then the questions began.

"How," asked the man, "is the crater of a volcano created?"

"Um," said Jackie. He looked at me, but I couldn't help him. "Um," he said again. "I don't know." At least he didn't admit that I'd practically done the project for him.

"Well … what happens to the lava when it has flowed out of the crater?" asked one of the women.

"It—it's very hot…" Jackie said lamely.

I looked at the ground. This was my fault. I felt terrible as I watched the judges make notations on their pads of paper. They walked on to the last project of the fair without even telling Jackie, "Good work," or "Nice going."

I went back to my parents and waited guiltily and nervously for the results of the fair to be announced.

"Jackie's project was great!" Dad said to me. "I've never seen such a thing. You really helped him."

A little too much, I thought.

Several minutes later, another announcement crackled over the loudspeaker. "The judges," said the principal, "have reached their decisions." (The judges were standing in the center of the room.) "They have chosen first-, second-, and third-place winners. When the winners are announced, will they please receive their ribbons from the judges? Thank you." There was a pause. Then the principal continued. "Third prize goes to Charlotte Johanssen for her project entitled 'The Power of Music.'"

**JUST THE FACTS**

When is Jessi's birthday? What color is Jackie Rodowsky's hair? Editors of the BSC can answer these questions in the blink of an eye. They just look in their special book that lists ALL the facts about the characters in the series.

Applause broke out. Charlotte, looking shy but pleased, edged over to the judges, received her yellow ribbon, and scurried back to her table, where she proudly attached the ribbon to the sign she'd made for her project.

The next two winners were announced. They went to kids I didn't know. I sought out Kristy, Mal, and my other friends in the crowd. Except for Stacey, they looked as disappointed as I felt.

But nobody looked more disappointed than Jackie, even though an Honorable Mention ribbon was already being fastened to his desk. (Every kid except the three winners was given an Honorable Mention.) The Rodowskys and I crowded around The World of Volcanic Activity.

"Don't be too upset, honey," Mrs. Rodowsky told Jackie.

I had to speak up. "He has a right to be upset," I said.

Mr. and Mrs. Rodowsky turned to me. "Why?" they asked at the same time.

"Because—because I gave him so much help with his project that he really didn't do much of it himself."

"Yeah," said Jackie, giving me the evil eyeball.

"I'm really sorry," I went on. "I just wanted him to win. He's always saying he's no good at anything, or that he has bad luck. I wanted him to see that he *can* be a winner. I guess I went about it all wrong, though."

Mr. and Mrs. Rodowsky were really nice. They understood what had happened. I got the feeling that they might have done things like this for Jackie in the past. Mr. Rodowsky even admitted to building the glass and wood box for the volcano himself. (Well, with a *teeny* bit of help from Jackie.)

But Jackie, who's usually so easygoing and sunny, continued to scowl at me. "I just wanted to have fun," he said. "That was all. I just wanted to make a volcano erupt."

"Jackie, Jessi apologized to you," his father said gently.

"I know." Jackie finally managed a smile. But it quickly turned to a frown. "Oh, no," he muttered. "Here come John, Ian, and Danny. They're going to laugh at me. I just know it."

But the three boys who approached us looked excited.

"Jackie," said one, "your volcano was totally rad. Make it explode again!"

"Yeah," said another. "That was so cool."

Jackie explained why he couldn't "explode" the volcano again.

"Oh, well," said the boys. "It was still awesome."

They started to walk away. "See you in school on Monday!" one called over his shoulder.

Jackie grinned at me like the Cheshire Cat. "I don't believe it!" he cried.

Mr. and Mrs. Rodowsky were smiling, too. "You know," said Jackie's mom, "there'll be another science fair next year. Jessi, maybe you could try helping Jackie again."

"I don't think so," I said. "I better not."

"Good," replied Jackie. "Because if I'm going to lose, I want to do it all by myself!"

## How to
# Make a Character Fact File

the series in which the character appears ●...........

the character's name ●...........

age ●...........

what the ● ........
character looks like

**A**uthors of hit series have fantastic imaginations! They create characters that appear in books, TV series, comics, or even video games. How do series authors keep track of the characters they create? One way is to make a fact file for each character.

**What is a character fact file?** A character fact file tells important details about a character.

**SERIES:**
The Baby-sitters Club

**CHARACTER:**
Jackie Rodowsky

- seven years old
- red hair, red cheeks, freckles
- big grin, with one tooth missing
- has two brothers, Shea and Archie
- loses tooth playing ball; likes losing teeth
- hits a home run and breaks the window of his elementary school
- baby-sitter, Jessi, helps him make a working volcano for the science fair; but she does most of the work
- is called the "walking disaster"
- is accident-prone
- plays the kazoo in a band that the Baby-sitters Club organizes
- has a pet grasshopper named Elizabeth

**facts about the character's family**

**important events in the character's life**

**other details about the character**

# 1 Create a Character

Think of a hit series you like. Then make up a new character who can appear in the series. You might create a new superhero, a girl detective who helps Encyclopedia Brown, a new neighbor for Charlie Brown, a cat who helps Lassie, or a new friend for Ramona Quimby. There are hundreds of series in need of new characters.

**TOOLS**

- pencil and paper
- colored pencils or marking pens

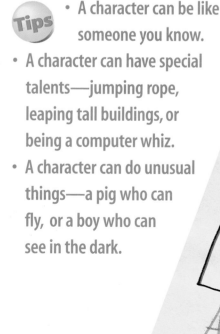

Angela the Detective

**Tips**
- A character can be like someone you know.
- A character can have special talents—jumping rope, leaping tall buildings, or being a computer whiz.
- A character can do unusual things—a pig who can fly, or a boy who can see in the dark.

# 2 List Character Facts

What is your character like? These questions can help you think of details about your character. Jot down your ideas.

- In which series will this character appear?
- What is the character's name?
- What does the character look like?
- Where does the character live?
- What hobbies does the character have?
- Is the character funny, serious, friendly, helpful, or playful?

The Robot Roberto

# 3 Make a Fact File

Now you can make a character fact file. At the top of a sheet of paper, write the character's name. Below the name, write all the information you have made up about the character. Be sure to include the series in which the character will appear. If you wish, draw a picture of your character on a separate sheet of paper. Put it with the character's fact file.

# 4 Discuss Your Character

You have written down a lot of information about the character you created. Now let your classmates read your character fact file. Answer questions about the character. Compare the character to the ones your classmates have created. Will any of the characters appear in the same series?

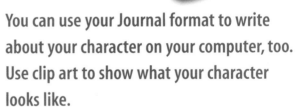

## If You Are Using a Computer ...

You can use your Journal format to write about your character on your computer, too. Use clip art to show what your character looks like.

**THINK**

Writers often put bits of themselves into characters. How is the character that you just created similar to or different from the real you?

Joanna Cole and
Bruce Degen
*Author and Illustrator* ▶

There are many different kinds of series.

# A Series for Everyone

Get the facts about insects from a series that features fabulous photos.

Figure out some picture riddles. Then learn how the eye-catching photographic clues are created.

Join a famous boy detective as he solves a mystery. Track down a cartoon criminal who's a hit in a computer game and on TV.

# Workshop 2

Review your favorite hit series.

CREATIVE EXPRESSION

ANTWON BUTLER
age 8

LITTLE HOUSE IN THE BIG WOODS

# *from* Incredible

## Hard cases

There are more kinds of beetles than any other animal in the world. We know of about 300,000 species so far, compared to only 4,500 species of mammals.

Ladybug

**Tiny giraffe**

The giraffe weevil is a type of beetle with a very long neck. Nobody knows why it is this shape.

*A neck twice as long as its body*

Giraffe weevil

*Beetles have tough wing cases that shield most of their bodies.*

# Mini-Beasts

by
Christopher Maynard

## Spot the spots

The ladybug is a bright red beetle speckled with black spots. These spots warn birds that ladybugs taste absolutely awful.

*Powerful jaws for biting and chewing*

## Mouth on a pole

Many weevils' jaws are on the end of a long snout. This makes it easy for them to drill holes through wood and nuts.

Frog beetle

*Grabbing a bite to eat*

## Frog march

Frog beetles have strong back legs that they use to leap away from danger—just like frogs. Once clear, they unfold their hind wings and fly away to safety.

*Beetles use their hind legs to take off.*

55

# Munching machines

Caterpillars are eating machines.
A single one can polish off every leaf on
a bush during just a few days of nonstop
feasting.

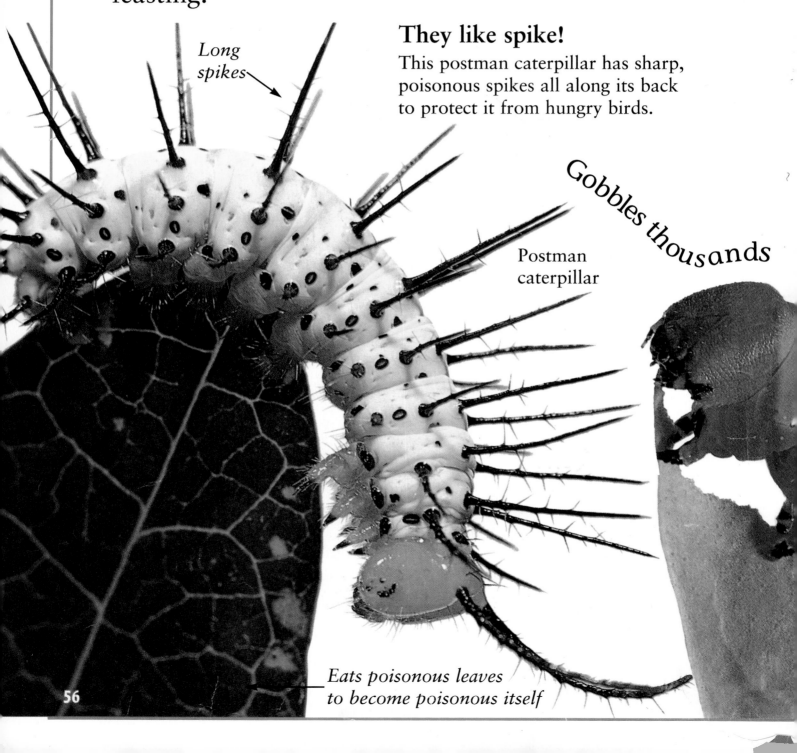

*Long
spikes*

**They like spike!**
This postman caterpillar has sharp,
poisonous spikes all along its back
to protect it from hungry birds.

Gobbles thousands

Postman
caterpillar

*Eats poisonous leaves
to become poisonous itself*

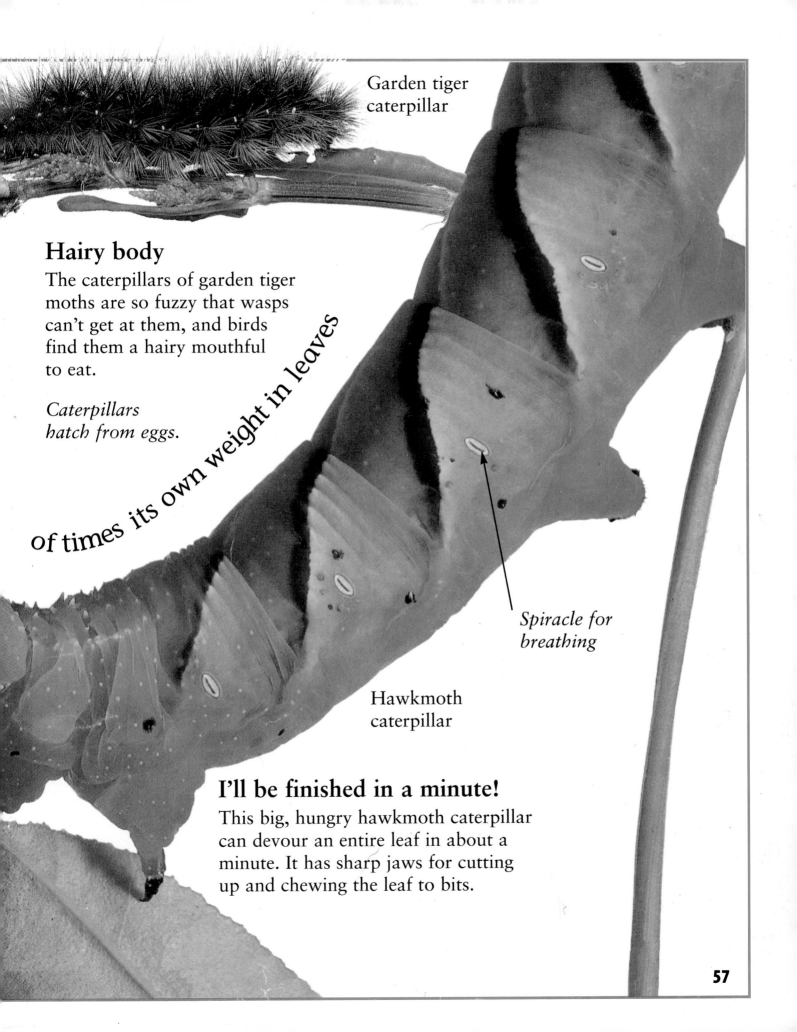

Garden tiger
caterpillar

## Hairy body

The caterpillars of garden tiger
moths are so fuzzy that wasps
can't get at them, and birds
find them a hairy mouthful
to eat.

*Caterpillars
hatch from eggs.*

of times its own weight in leaves

*Spiracle for
breathing*

Hawkmoth
caterpillar

## I'll be finished in a minute!

This big, hungry hawkmoth caterpillar
can devour an entire leaf in about a
minute. It has sharp jaws for cutting
up and chewing the leaf to bits.

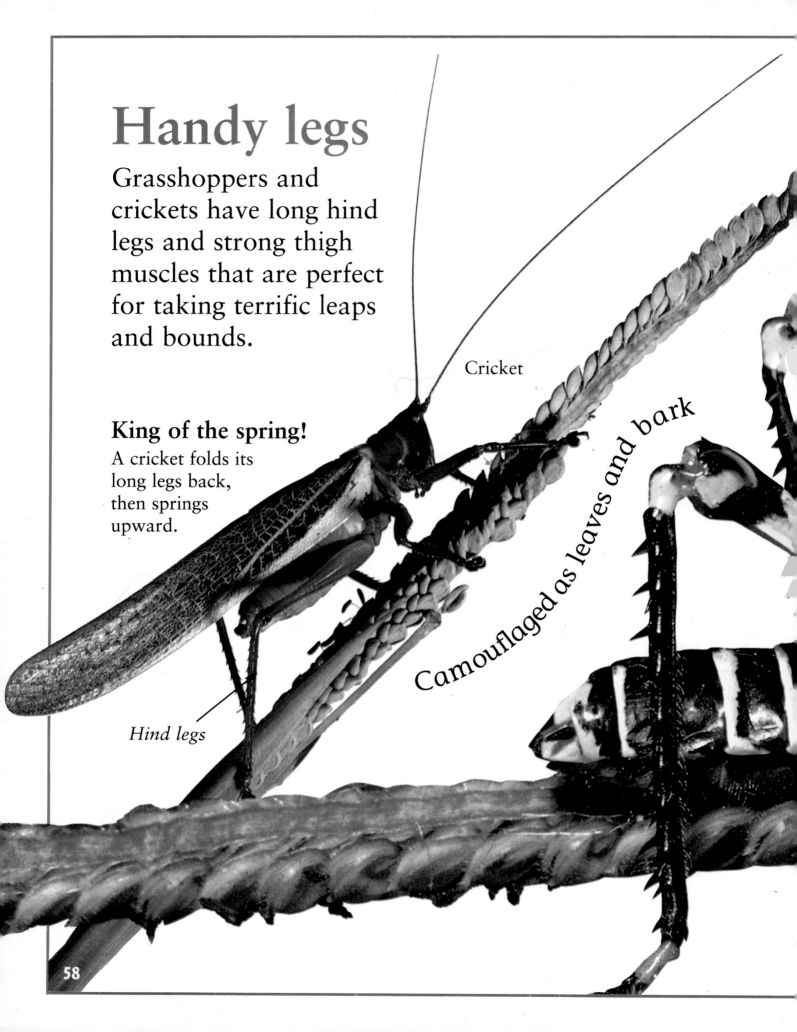

# Handy legs

Grasshoppers and crickets have long hind legs and strong thigh muscles that are perfect for taking terrific leaps and bounds.

Cricket

**King of the spring!**
A cricket folds its long legs back, then springs upward.

*Hind legs*

Camouflaged as leaves and bark

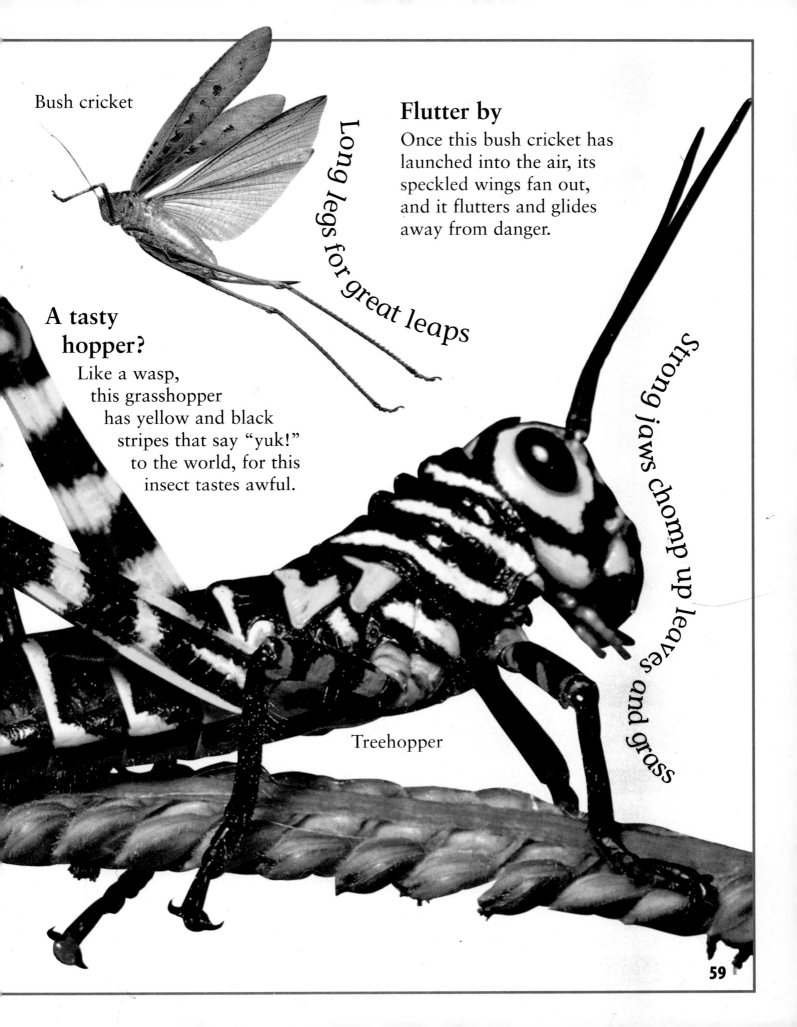

Bush cricket

Long legs for great leaps

## Flutter by

Once this bush cricket has launched into the air, its speckled wings fan out, and it flutters and glides away from danger.

## A tasty hopper?

Like a wasp, this grasshopper has yellow and black stripes that say "yuk!" to the world, for this insect tastes awful.

Strong jaws chomp up leaves and grass

Treehopper

# Seriously deadly

A hairy tarantula may be scary to look at, but watch out for its bite! It is deadly to birds and small animals, but only as bad as a bee sting to human beings.

Look out for a spider that's big and hairy!

Tarantula

**Call me spike!**
This strange spider has spikes around its body. It is too prickly for hunters to pick up.

Spike spider

*I'm a spiky spinner*

**Fangs for everything**
The tarantula's fangs inject paralyzing poison. Food is eaten quickly, still alive and fresh!

*Stinger*

*Whiplash tail with a long sharp sting*

Scorpion

*Eight legs like a spider*

**Tails of poison**
The scorpion, a relative of the spider, has a poisonous stinger in its tail. Most scorpions are harmless, but the desert scorpion can kill a person with its sting.

*Pincers for catching food*

from

# I SPY

**Photographs by Walter Wick**
**Riddles by Jean Marzollo**

I spy a shovel, a long silver chain,
A little toy horse, a track for a train;

A birthday candle, a pretty gold ring,
A small puzzle piece, and a crown for a king.

I spy a turtle, a penny for a wish,
A door ajar, and a jewelry fish;

Four anchors, a ship, a shadowy whale,
A pot of gold, and A MERMAID'S TALE.

# THE MAKING OF I SPY

*It takes a quick mind and a sharp eye,*
*To bring you the series that's known as I SPY!*

Jean Marzollo and Walter Wick
put their talents together in the
eye-catching *I SPY* series.

## Getting Started

Each book begins with Jean Marzollo and Walter Wick discussing a theme and brainstorming ideas for the photos. Then Wick goes looking for objects for the photographs.

The number of items needed for each photo is mind-boggling! Wick's search takes him to flea markets, crafts shops, toy stores, and even friends' attics.

Wick sets up
the shot.

**Everything is in place.**

## Shooting *I SPY*

To create one of the photographs for *I SPY Fun House,* Wick first built a wooden frame. From it he hung shiny musical instruments. Next he glued cut-out musical notes onto a white wall. Special lights made the wall look blue.

Wick placed colorful toy clowns above the instruments so they would be reflected in the horns. It took several days for everything to look just right. When it did, Wick shot the picture. Lights! Camera! Click!

**This is "Circus Band," one of the photos that appeared in *I SPY Fun House.***

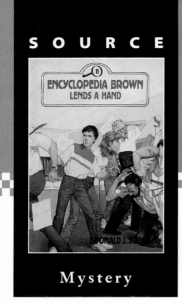

from
# ENCYCLOPEDIA BROWN
LENDS A HAND

THE
# CASE of the
# RUNAWAY
# ELEPHANT

## by Donald J. Sobol

### illustrated by Leonard Shortall

. . . . . . . . . . . . . . . . . . . . . . . . . . . . . .

**A**cross the length and breadth of America people were wondering:

"What is Idaville's secret?"

For more than a year now, no one had gotten away with a crime in Idaville.

Aside from being a model of law and order, Idaville was a lovely seaside town. It had clean beaches and three movie theaters. It had churches, a synagogue, four banks, and two delicatessens.

The chief of police was Mr. Brown. He knew that nearly every American thought he was the best peace officer in the nation. He also knew the truth about Idaville.

The real brains behind Idaville's war on crime was his only child, ten-year-old Encyclopedia.

Whenever Chief Brown had a mystery he could not solve, he put his emergency plan into action. He went home to dinner. At the table he told Encyclopedia the facts.

The boy detective solved the case before dessert. Once in a while, however, he had to ask for second helpings to gain more time.

Chief Brown hated keeping his son's ability a secret. He felt Congress should award Encyclopedia a vote of thanks. But how could he suggest it?

Who would believe that the guiding hand behind Idaville's police record could make a yo-yo loop-the-loop off a man-on-the-flying trapeze?

"Mr. Hunt opened his eyes, and there was Jimbo peeping through the window."

No one.

So Chief Brown said nothing.

Encyclopedia never let slip a word about the help he gave his father. He did not want to seem different from other fifth-graders.

But he was stuck with his nickname.

Only his parents and teachers called him by his right name, Leroy. Everyone else in Idaville called him Encyclopedia.

An encyclopedia is a book or set of books filled with facts from A to Z. Encyclopedia had read so many books he was really more like a library. You might say he was the only library in which the information desk was on the top floor.

One evening Chief Brown looked up from his soup. "Friday the thirteenth," he muttered.

"You're mistaken, dear," said Mrs. Brown. "Today is Friday the twelfth."

"I'm talking about seventeen years ago," said Chief Brown.

"Does the date have something to do with a case?" asked Encyclopedia.

"Yes, with Mr. Hunt's elephant, Jimbo," answered Chief Brown. "The animal is causing a problem."

Encyclopedia refused to believe his ears. Jimbo was the only pet elephant in Idaville. He never caused anyone a problem. Mr. Hunt kept him in the backyard.

"If Jimbo is in the middle of a mystery, tell Leroy," urged Mrs. Brown. "It could be his biggest case."

Chief Brown nodded. "It turns out that Jimbo may not belong to Mr. Hunt after all," he began. "Mr. Hunt found him outside his bedroom window on April Fools' Day seventeen years ago."

"What a shock for him!" exclaimed Mrs. Brown.

"I imagine so," replied Chief Brown. "Mr. Hunt opened his eyes, and there was Jimbo peeping through the window. He woke up Mrs. Hunt to make sure he wasn't dreaming."

"What did she say?" asked Encyclopedia.

" 'I hope he's on a leash,' " replied Chief Brown, "according to Mr. Hunt."

"Mr. Hunt has a great memory," marveled Encyclopedia.

"So does Mr. Xippas," said Chief Brown. "He came to my office today. He says he owns the elephant and wants him back. He claims Mr. Hunt never paid for Jimbo."

"What does Mr. Hunt say?" inquired Mrs. Brown.

"Mr. Hunt insists that he mailed the money to Mr. Xippas," said Chief Brown.

He waited while Mrs. Brown cleared the soup bowls. When she had served the ham loaf, he took his notebook from his breast pocket.

"I spoke with both Mr. Xippas and Mr. Hunt today," he said. "I'll give you Mr. Hunt's side first."

Encyclopedia and his mother listened as Chief Brown read from his notes.

**IT'S A FACT!**

Donald Sobol's first book about Encyclopedia Brown was turned down by 26 publishers.

"Mr. Hunt says that he thought the elephant in his backyard was a prank, since it was April Fools' Day. He immediately called the police. It turned out that the elephant had run away from a little circus which had just arrived in town.

"An hour later Mr. Xippas came to Mr. Hunt's house. Mr. Xippas owned and trained Jimbo. By then the Hunts had taken a liking to the animal. They asked Mr. Xippas if he would sell him.

"Mr. Xippas agreed. He also agreed to stay at the Hunts' house a week or two. The couple wanted to learn how to care for Jimbo. Mr. Xippas, however, asked to see their money first. So that afternoon Mr. Hunt drew the cash from the Oceanside Bank and showed it to the animal trainer.

"After nearly two weeks, the Hunts felt they could handle the friendly Jimbo. Mr. Hunt offered Mr. Xippas the money. Mr. Xippas wouldn't take it because it was Friday the thirteenth, which he said was bad luck for him.

"The same night Mr. Xippas left Idaville. He left a forwarding address, and Mr. Hunt mailed him the money."

Chief Brown looked up from his notebook.

"That's Mr. Hunt's story," he said. "Mr. Xippas insists he never got the money. The address was his sister's house in New Jersey. He says she was sick and had telephoned him to come and be with her."

"Why did Mr. Xippas wait seventeen years before coming back to Idaville to claim Jimbo?" asked Encyclopedia. "It doesn't sound right."

"He says his sister died shortly after he reached her bedside," replied Chief Brown. "A day after her death, he got an offer of a job in India. He's been overseas all this time. He only returned to the United States five days ago."

"I wonder about him," said Mrs. Brown. "Why did he ask to see Mr. Hunt's money that very first day? I don't think that was nice. He should have trusted Mr. Hunt."

"Mr. Xippas says he didn't ask to see the money," answered Chief Brown. "He says Mr. Hunt never went to the bank. Furthermore, the only reason he stayed so long with the Hunts was that every day Mr. Hunt promised to pay him the following day."

Chief Brown closed his notebook.

"I should add," he said, "that Mr. Xippas denies that he refused the money on Friday the thirteenth because it was bad luck. He says the only thing Mr. Hunt gave him were promises to pay."

"What about the bank?" said Mrs. Brown. "Don't banks keep records?"

"A hurricane struck later that year," said Chief Brown. "It flooded the Oceanside Bank, Mr. Hunt's home, and most of the buildings in Idaville. All the records were destroyed."

"I still don't understand something," said Mrs. Brown. "Mr. Xippas worked in the circus. How could he take nearly two weeks off to stay with the Hunts?"

"Mr. Xippas told me that he had become tired of circus life," said Chief Brown. "By selling Jimbo, he could quit and open his own business."

"Whom to believe?" sighed Mrs. Brown.

She had risen to clear the dishes and bring in the dessert. She glanced at Encyclopedia with concern. He always solved a case before dessert. Was this case too hard?

The boy detective closed his eyes. He always closed his eyes when he did his deepest thinking.

Suddenly his eyes opened. "Dad," he said. "Both men have memories like an elephant. But the one who is lying is Mr.——"

WHO?

*Turn the page*

*for the*
**solution** *to*
the case.

# SOLUTION TO THE CASE of the RUNAWAY ELEPHANT

**M**r. Hunt never paid for the elephant.

He lied when he said Mr. Xippas refused to accept payment on Friday the thirteenth because it was bad luck.

But what tripped him up was another lie. He said he had gone to the bank on April Fools' Day and had drawn out the money to buy Jimbo. Impossible!

Because it happened seventeen years ago, he thought he was safe. He had not reckoned on Encyclopedia.

April Fools' Day is April 1.

As Encyclopedia knew, if in any month a Friday falls on the thirteenth, the first day of the month is Sunday.

On Sundays banks are closed.

*from*

# 101 Elephant JokeS

*Compiled by* **ROBERT BLAKE**

SOURCE

101 ELEPHANT JOKES

Joke Book

*Illustrated by* **PETER SPACEK**

## Why are **elephants** trumpeters?

It is too hard for them to learn to play the piano!

## Why do **elephants** wear **blue** sneakers?

Their red ones are in the laundry!

## Why do **elephants** wear sneakers while jumping from tree to tree?

They don't want to wake up the neighbors!

## What time is it when an **elephant** sits on a fence?

Time to buy a new fence!

## What's **gray** and **white** and **red** all over?

An embarrassed elephant!

## Where do you find **elephants**?

It depends on where you leave them!

# Where in the World is Carmen Sandiego?®

## BY CHARLES NORDLANDER

## All in the Game

Carmen Sandiego started her career in 1985 in the computer game called *Where in the World is Carmen Sandiego?®* Game players chased her all over the world. And sometimes, they even caught her!

Carmen Sandiego, in case you haven't heard, is the fictional leader of a bunch of thieves. Carmen and her crew nab famous buildings, monuments, and islands, too. Even the Empire State Building and the Grand Canyon aren't safe when Carmen is nearby.

Kids use their wits, knowledge of geography, and computer skills to catch the slippery leader.

A California company that makes computer software created Carmen Sandiego. The first game was such a big hit that many sequels followed. One version of the game even sends players into outer space to track her! And there's a Junior Detective Edition for gumshoes eight years old and younger.

Stretch the Crime Dog has a good nose for catching criminals.

## TV Star

Carmen made her big jump to television in 1991 in the PBS series *Where in the World Is Carmen Sandiego?*® For the first time, kids without computers had a chance to catch her. At the same time, Carmen was making music news. Rockapella, the singing group who appears on the show, had people everywhere humming the Carmen Sandiego theme song.

As a TV star, Carmen Sandiego was not any easier to catch, but she certainly became easier to see. She began showing up everywhere—in record stores, in books and magazines, and even on backpacks.

◄ **Carmine the Cat is a purr-fect member of Carmen's team.**

ROCKAPELLA CENTER

NORD EXPRESS

WHERE IN THE WORLD IS CARMEN SANDIEGO?

TITO PUENTE
THE PERSUASIONS

ROCKAPELLA

URBAN BLIGHT
3 BRAVE WOODSMEN

◀ Carmen Sandiego recordings hit stores in 1992, with songs by the TV show's singing group, Rockapella.

Bad guys beware! Computer players get help from ACME Detective Agency crime-fighters Penelope Paparazzi and F-Stop Freddy.
▼

◀ On the TV show, guest detectives and host Greg Lee give Carmen a run for her money. Six million kids a week tune in to watch.

### Charles Nordlander

is the head
scriptwriter for the
Carmen Sandiego
live-game show
on PBS. He has
written more than
245 episodes. Like
Carmen, he loves
to travel. Unlike
Carmen, he leaves
things where he
finds them!

## A Real Page-Turner

Where do the facts on the Carmen Sandiego TV show come from? The folks at *National Geographic World*, a children's magazine, gather and check all material used on the show. But that's not all. The editors at the magazine decided it was time for Carmen to appear in print. In September 1992, Carmen became a monthly comic strip in their magazine.

## The Future

What's next for Carmen? Well, she has been spotted in books, puzzles, a board game, a calendar, and more. Soon gumshoes may even be chasing her across a movie screen! One thing's for sure: Carmen will have to get faster and smarter to stay ahead of the kids on her trail.

# Hail to the Chief!

**Lynne Thigpen** plays the role of The Chief of Acme Crimenet on the PBS television show, *Where in the World Is Carmen Sandiego?* Here's what she has to say about the series:

"Why is *Carmen Sandiego* such a big hit with kids? First of all, it's fun. All kids like to have fun! But Carmen is more than that. The show gives kids credit for what they've *learned*. In fact, a lot of adults don't know the things that kids on *Carmen* know.

"A father told me about the birthday present his son wanted. He asked for large maps to hang by his bed. I was so thrilled that *Carmen Sandiego* could have that kind of effect!"

## How to
# Write a Series Review

author of
the series

**H**ow did you discover your favorite hit series? Did a friend tell you about it? Did you read a glowing review about it in a newspaper or magazine?

a favorite
scene

**What is a review?** A review is one person's opinion about a book, movie, cartoon, comic book, TV show, video game, or some other kind of entertainment.

how the
reviewer
feels about
the book

LITTLE HOUSE ON THE PRAIRIE · LAURA INGALLS WILDER

LITTLE HOUSE IN THE BIG WOODS · LAURA INGALLS WILD

**name of reviewer**

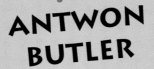

**ANTWON BUTLER**

age 8

title of the review names one book in the series

where and when the story takes place

# LITTLE HOUSE IN THE BIG WOODS

Laura Ingalls Wilder is the author of *Little House in the Big Woods* and also its main character. This first book in the Little House series is about the Ingalls family, who lived in a cabin in northern Wisconsin a long time ago. I especially liked one chapter called "Dance at Grandpa's." Grandma dances and even beats Uncle George in a dance called a jig. I could picture that in my mind, and it made me laugh. The book also tells you how to make maple syrup.

ILLUSTRATED BY GARTH WILLIAMS

When I finished reading this book, I was sad it was over. So I read the rest of the series. I think people should read these books because you find out that even though Laura lived many years ago she was still a kid, and kids will always have things in common.

# 1 Choose a Series

Choose a series to review. If you can't think of a series, ask a friend, teacher, or librarian to suggest a good one. Then gather several books, cartoons, or comics in the series. If you are reviewing a TV or movie series, jot down the titles of some episodes you have seen.

TOOLS

• pencil and paper

# 2 Make Notes

Make some notes about the series you have chosen. Here are some questions to help you:

- Is it a series you read or one that you watch?

- Is the series fiction or nonfiction? If it's fiction, what kind of story is it? If it's nonfiction, what topic does it tell about?

- What's the same in each book or episode? What's different?

- Who are your favorite characters? Why?

- Which book or episode do you want to review?

# 3 Write Your Review

Use your notes to write your review. Include the title of the episode, the series it came from, and the author. Tell what the series is about. Don't forget to describe an important scene from one episode. Be sure to tell your readers how you feel about the series. Last, but not least, sign your review, so everyone will know who wrote it.

# 4 Share Your Review

Read your review aloud to your classmates, and answer any questions they have. For anyone who is interested, you can suggest other favorite books or episodes in the series.

## If You Are Using a Computer ...

Write your review in the Newsletter format. Create a headline. Use clip art so your review looks like a newspaper article.

**Tip** How do you rate the series you just reviewed? Was it fantastic, great, good, or just okay? Write your rating at the top of your review.

**THINK**
Reviewers tell their opinions about books, TV, movies, and music. Why do you think it's important to read these reviews?

Joanna Cole and
Bruce Degen
*Author and Illustrator* ▶

# Long-Running Hits

Meet adventure with the Ingalls family as they travel to a new "little house." Then explore a place where Laura once played.

Visit the old Southwest and discover a chile-flavored version of *The Three Little Pigs*.

## PROJECT

Create an episode for a hit series.

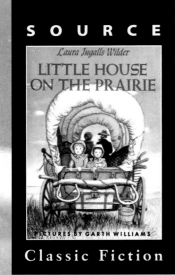
from

# LITTLE HOUSE on the PRAIRIE

by Laura Ingalls Wilder
illustrated by Garth Williams

AWARD WINNING

Book

The Big Woods was getting too crowded. It was time to move West. So the Ingalls family—Pa, Ma, Mary, Laura, and baby Carrie—packed their belongings into a covered wagon and hitched up the horses, Pet and Patty. With Jack, their dog, trotting under the wagon, they began the long journey to a new home on the prairie.

Many miles later, the family was glad to see a good spot for camping among some trees ahead.

**P**et and Patty began to trot briskly, as if they were glad, too. Laura held tight to the wagon bow and stood up in the jolting wagon. Beyond Pa's shoulder and far across the waves of green grass she could see the trees, and they were not like any trees she had seen before. They were no taller than bushes.

"Whoa!" said Pa, suddenly. "Now which way?" he muttered to himself.

The road divided here, and you could not tell which was the more-traveled way. Both of them were faint wheel tracks in the grass. One went toward the west, the other sloped downward a little, toward the south. Both soon vanished in the tall, blowing grass.

"Better go downhill, I guess," Pa decided. "The creek's down in the bottoms. Must be this is the way to the ford." He turned Pet and Patty toward the south.

The road went down and up and down and up again, over gently curving land. The trees were nearer now, but they were no taller. Then Laura gasped and clutched the wagon bow, for almost under Pet's and Patty's noses there was no more blowing grass, there was no land at all. She looked beyond the edge of the land and across the tops of trees.

The road turned there. For a little way it went
along the cliff's top, then it went sharply downward.
Pa put on the brakes; Pet and Patty braced themselves
backward and almost sat down. The wagon wheels slid
onward, little by little lowering the wagon farther
down the steep slope into the ground. Jagged cliffs of
bare red earth rose up on both sides of the wagon.
Grass waved along their tops, but nothing grew on
their seamed, straight-up-and-down sides. They were
hot, and heat came from them against Laura's face.
The wind was still blowing overhead, but it did not
blow into this deep crack in the ground. The stillness
seemed strange and empty.

Then once more the wagon was level. The narrow crack down which it had come opened into the bottom lands. Here grew the tall trees whose tops Laura had seen from the prairie above. Shady groves were scattered on the rolling meadows, and in the groves deer were lying down, hardly to be seen among the shadows. The deer turned their heads toward the wagon, and curious fawns stood up to see it more clearly.

Laura was surprised because she did not see the creek. But the bottom lands were wide. Down here, below the prairie, there were gentle hills and open sunny places. The air was still and hot. Under the wagon wheels the ground was soft. In the sunny open spaces the grass grew thin, and deer had cropped it short.

For a while the high, bare cliffs of red earth stood up behind the wagon. But they were almost hidden behind hills and trees when Pet and Patty stopped to drink from the creek.

The rushing sound of the water filled the still air. All along the creek banks the trees hung over it and made it dark with shadows. In the middle it ran swiftly, sparkling silver and blue.

"This creek's pretty high," Pa said. "But I guess we can make it all right. You can see this is a ford, by the old wheel ruts. What do you say, Caroline?"

"Whatever you say, Charles," Ma answered.

Pet and Patty lifted their wet noses. They pricked their ears forward, looking at the creek; then they pricked them backward to hear what Pa would say. They sighed and laid their soft noses together to whisper to each other. A little way upstream, Jack was lapping the water with his red tongue.

## STARTING OUT

*Little House in the Big Woods* was Laura Ingalls Wilder's first book in the series. She wrote it when she was 63 years old.

"I'll tie down the wagon-cover," Pa said. He climbed down from the seat, unrolled the canvas sides and tied them firmly to the wagon box. Then he pulled the rope at the back, so that the canvas puckered together in the middle, leaving only a tiny round hole, too small to see through.

Mary huddled down on the bed. She did not like fords; she was afraid of the rushing water. But Laura was excited; she liked the splashing. Pa climbed to the seat, saying, "They may have to swim, out there in the middle. But we'll make it all right, Caroline."

Laura thought of Jack and said, "I wish Jack could ride in the wagon, Pa."

Pa did not answer. He gathered the reins tightly in his hands. Ma said "Jack can swim, Laura. He will be all right."

The wagon went forward softly in mud. Water began to splash against the wheels. The splashing grew louder. The wagon shook as the noisy water struck at it. Then all at once the wagon lifted and balanced and swayed. It was a lovely feeling.

The noise stopped, and Ma said, sharply, "Lie down, girls!"

Quick as a flash, Mary and Laura dropped flat on the bed. When Ma spoke like that, they did as they were told. Ma's arm pulled a smothering blanket over them, heads and all.

"Be still, just as you are. Don't move!" she said.

Mary did not move; she was trembling and still.

But Laura could not help wriggling a little bit. She did so want to see what was happening. She could feel the wagon swaying and turning; the splashing was noisy again, and again it died away. Then Pa's voice frightened Laura. It said, "Take them, Caroline!"

The wagon lurched; there was a sudden heavy splash beside it. Laura sat straight up and clawed the blanket from her head.

Pa was gone. Ma sat alone, holding tight to the reins with both hands. Mary hid her face in the blanket again, but Laura rose up farther. She couldn't see the creek bank. She couldn't see anything in front of the wagon but water rushing at it. And in the water, three heads; Pet's head and Patty's head and Pa's small, wet head. Pa's fist in the water was holding tight to Pet's bridle.

Laura could faintly hear Pa's voice through the rushing of the water. It sounded calm and cheerful, but she couldn't hear what he said. He was talking to the horses. Ma's face was white and scared.

"Lie down, Laura," Ma said.

Laura lay down. She felt cold and sick. Her eyes were shut tight, but she could still see the terrible water and Pa's brown beard drowning in it.

For a long, long time the wagon swayed and swung, and Mary cried without making a sound, and Laura's stomach felt sicker and sicker. Then the front wheels struck and grated, and Pa shouted. The whole wagon jerked and jolted and tipped backward, but the wheels were turning on the ground. Laura was up again, holding to the seat; she saw Pet's and Patty's scrambling wet backs climbing a steep bank, and Pa running beside them, shouting, "Hi, Patty! Hi, Pet! Get up! Get up! Whoopsy-daisy!  Good girls!"

At the top of the bank they stood still, panting and dripping. And the wagon stood still, safely out of that creek.

Pa stood panting and dripping, too, and Ma said, "Oh, Charles!"

"There, there, Caroline," said Pa. "We're all safe, thanks to a good tight wagon-box well fastened to the running-gear. I never saw a creek rise so fast in my life. Pet and Patty are good swimmers, but I guess they wouldn't have made it if I hadn't helped them."

## ANOTHER HIT SERIES

The Little House books became a hit television series, too.  Thousands of viewers began following the adventures of the Ingalls family in 1974.

If Pa had not known what to do, or if Ma had been too frightened to drive, or if Laura and Mary had been naughty and bothered her, then they would all have been lost. The river would have rolled them over and over and carried them away and drowned them, and nobody would ever have known what became of them. For weeks, perhaps, no other person would come along that road.

"Well," said Pa, "all's well that ends well," and Ma said, "Charles, you're wet to the skin."

Before Pa could answer, Laura cried, "Oh, where's Jack?"

They had forgotten Jack. They had left him on the other side of that dreadful water and now they could not see him anywhere. He must have tried to swim after them, but they could not see him struggling in the water now.

Laura swallowed hard, to keep from crying. She knew it was shameful to cry, but there was crying inside her. All the long way from Wisconsin poor Jack had followed them so patiently and faithfully, and now they had left him to drown. He was so tired, and they might have taken him into the wagon. He had stood on the bank and seen the wagon going away from him, as if they didn't care for him at all. And he would never know how much they wanted him.

Pa said he wouldn't have done such a thing to Jack, not for a million dollars. If he'd known how that creek would rise when they were in mid-stream, he would never have let Jack try to swim it. "But that can't be helped now," he said.

He went far up and down the creek bank, looking for Jack, calling him and whistling for him.

It was no use. Jack was gone.

Was Jack *really* swept away in the creek? Don't be kept in suspense! Read the rest of this exciting book to find out.

SOURCE

Travel Diary

104

# SEARCHING FOR LAURA INGALLS

## A Reader's Journey

### by Kathryn Lasky and Meribah Knight
### photographs by Christopher G. Knight

Meribah Knight loved all of Laura Ingalls Wilder's *Little House* books. And she wanted to visit Laura's many homes more than anything. One summer Meribah's wish came true. She and her family traveled by camper to some of the places Laura Ingalls had lived, including Plum Creek in western Minnesota.

In 1873 the Ingalls family had moved from Wisconsin to a dugout house that was built near Plum Creek. Laura was only six, and she couldn't swim. But she loved to wade in the creek on hot summer days and cool her toes in the clear water.

After Meribah read *On the Banks of Plum Creek*, she dreamed of swimming in the same creek where Laura had once waded. When Meribah arrived at Plum Creek, she put on an old-fashioned dress, just like one Laura once wore, and jumped in.

Here is how Meribah described Plum Creek in her diary.

◀ Meribah finds that this covered wagon, like the one Laura rode in, is very different from travel in a modern camper (above).

I finally had my dream come true, but it was almost a bad dream, a nightmare. I got to go wading and swimming in Plum Creek. ▼

It was warm and the current in the creek was going really fast. When I waded into the water I fell, but I got used to it and started to swim. When I stood up my clothes were heavy and wet. I felt like stones were hanging on my skirt. I climbed trees that were sticking out over the creek. ▶

◄ I remembered in the book how Laura went to look under branches and rocks for the old crab, the one she used to scare Nellie Oleson, the stuck-up girl in the book. I looked for it, too. I couldn't find it, so I swam along some more and hung from branches.

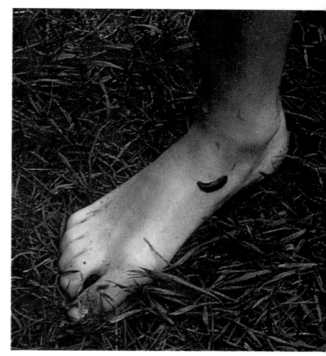

▲

But guess what? When I came out of Plum Creek I saw this thing that looked like a glob of mud on my foot, and then I thought, It's a black slug, but then I thought, Slugs aren't black. Then I remembered. It came back all awful. It was a leech just like the ones Laura got on her. I had forgotten this whole part of the book, the part about the leeches. My stomach flip-flopped, my brain went crazy, and I started to scream. Of course my dad just had to take a picture before he pulled it off me.

# THE THREE LITTLE JAVELINAS

by **Susan Lowell**
illustrated by **Jim Harris**

AWARD WINNING Book

**T**his is a southwestern adaptation of a familiar folk tale: a chile-flavored "The Three Little Pigs." The story takes place in the Sonoran Desert, where Native American, Mexican, and Anglo cultures blend together.

Javelina (pronounced ha-ve-LEE-na) comes from a Spanish name for the collared peccary, a relative of swine (but not a true pig). Javelinas are extremely bristly—very hairy on the chinny-chin-chin.

# ONCE UPON A TIME,

way out in the desert, there were three little javelinas. Javelinas (ha-ve-LEE-nas) are wild, hairy, southwestern cousins of pigs.

Their heads were hairy, their backs were hairy, and their bony legs—all the way down to their hard little hooves—were very hairy. But their snouts were soft and pink.

One day, the three little javelinas trotted away to seek their fortunes. In this hot, dry land, the sky was almost always blue. Steep purple mountains looked down on the desert, where the cactus forests grew.

Soon the little javelinas came to a spot where the path divided, and each one went a different way.

The first little javelina wandered lazily along. He didn't see a dust storm whirling across the desert—until it caught him.

The whirlwind blew away and left the first little javelina sitting in a heap of tumbleweeds. Brushing himself off, he said, "I'll build a house with them!" And in no time at all, he did.

Then along came a coyote. He ran through the desert so quickly and so quietly that he was almost invisible. In fact, this was only one of Coyote's many magical tricks. He laughed when he saw the tumbleweed house and smelled the javelina inside.

"Mmm! A tender juicy piggy!" he thought. Coyote was tired of eating mice and rabbits.

He called out sweetly, "Little pig, little pig, let me come in."

"Not by the hair of my chinny-chin-chin!" shouted the first javelina (who had a lot of hair on his chinny-chin-chin!)

"Then I'll huff, and I'll puff, and I'll blow your house in!" said Coyote.

And he huffed, and he puffed, and he blew the little tumbleweed house away.

But in all the hullabaloo, the first little javelina escaped—and went looking for his brother and sister.

Coyote, who was very sneaky, tiptoed along behind.

**112**

The second little javelina walked for miles among giant cactus plants called saguaros (sa-WA-ros). They held their ripe red fruit high in the sky. But they made almost no shade, and the little javelina grew hot.

Then he came upon a Native American woman who was gathering sticks from inside a dried-up cactus. She planned to use these long sticks, called saguaro ribs, to knock down the sweet cactus fruit.

The second little javelina said, "Please, may I have some sticks to build a house?"

"*Ha'u*," (Ha-ou) she said, which means "yes" in the language of the Desert People.

When he was finished building his house, he lay down in the shade. Then his brother arrived, panting from the heat, and the second little javelina moved over and made a place for him.

Pretty soon, Coyote found the saguaro rib house. He used his magic to make his voice sound just like another javelina's.

"Little pig, little pig, let me come in!" he called.

But the little javelinas were suspicious. The second one cried, "No! Not by the hair of my chinny-chin-chin!"

"Bah!" thought Coyote. "I am not going to eat your *hair.*"

Then Coyote smiled, showing all his sharp teeth: "I'll huff, and I'll puff, and I'll blow your house in!"

So he huffed, and he puffed, and all the saguaro ribs came tumbling down.

But the two little javelinas escaped into the desert.

Still not discouraged, Coyote followed. Sometimes his magic did fail, but then he usually came up with another trick.

The third little javelina trotted through beautiful palo verde trees, with green trunks and yellow flowers. She saw a snake sliding by, smooth as oil. A hawk floated round and round above her. Then she came to a place where a man was making adobe (a-DOE-be) bricks from mud and straw. The bricks lay on the ground, baking in the hot sun.

The third little javelina thought for a moment, and said, "May I please have a few adobes to build a house?"

"*Sí*," answered the man, which means "yes" in Spanish, the brick-maker's language.

So the third javelina built herself a solid little adobe house, cool in summer and warm in winter. When her brothers found her, she welcomed them in and locked the door behind them.

Coyote followed their trail.

"Little pig, little pig, let me come in!" he called.

The three little javelinas looked out the window. This time Coyote pretended to be very old and weak, with no teeth and a sore paw. But they were not fooled.

"No! Not by the hair of my chinny-chin-chin," called back the third little javelina.

"Then I'll huff, and I'll puff, and I'll blow your house in!" said Coyote. He grinned, thinking of the wild pig dinner to come.

"Just try it!" shouted the third little javelina.

So Coyote huffed and puffed, but the adobe bricks did not budge.

Again, Coyote tried. "I'LL HUFF...AND I'LL PUFF...AND I'LL BLOW YOUR HOUSE IN!"

The three little javelinas covered their hairy ears. But nothing happened. The javelinas peeked out the window.

The tip of Coyote's raggedy tail whisked right past their noses. He was climbing upon the tin roof. Next, Coyote used his magic to make himself very skinny.

"The stove pipe!" gasped the third little javelina. Quickly she lighted a fire inside her wood stove.

"What a feast it will be!" Coyote said to himself. He squeezed into the stove pipe. "I think I'll eat them with red hot chile sauce!"

Whoosh. S-s-sizzle!

Then the three little javelinas heard an amazing noise. It was not a bark. It was not a cackle. It was not a howl. It was not a scream. It was all of those sounds together.
"Yip
    yap
       yeep
           YEE-OWW-OOOOOOOOOOOOO!"
Away ran a puff of smoke shaped like a coyote.

The three little javelinas lived
happily ever after in the adobe house.
 And if you ever hear Coyote's voice,
way out in the desert at night. . .well,
you know what he's remembering!

# ...and still more Pigs

**T**his is the version of *The Three Little Pigs* that many grown-ups probably heard when they were young. Maybe it's the very first one that was told to you, too.

**H**ere's the old story with a new twist. It claims to be the inside lowdown on what *really* took place, as told to the author by none other than A. Wolf.

**T**hese pigs live in the Great Smoky Mountains of Appalachia. They seek their fortunes with corn dumplings and hoecakes in their sacks. Instead of a wolf, they've got to be on the lookout for the drooly-mouth fox who just lo-o-o-ves barbecued pig!

**N**ow here's a switch. The wolves in this version of the folk tale are the good guys! They need barbed wire and steel chains to keep out the villain—the very bad pig.

## How to
# Create a New Episode

**Write a story outline for a *new* episode *in a* series.**

**H**ooray! A new book in your favorite mystery series just arrived in the bookstore. How does the author keep writing new episodes? The answer is simple. It takes imagination and knowing what kids like. You can also find hit series on television, at the movies, in comics, and in cartoons. No matter where you look, there is always a new episode to read or watch.

# Look at a Series

**P**ut on your thinking cap. It's time to come up with an idea for a new episode in your favorite series. First, choose a fiction series you like. It can be a book, cartoon, or a comic strip series that you read, or a TV, movie, or computer game series that you watch.

**TOOLS**

- paper and pencil
- markers or colored pencils

Then, take a close look at the series. Answer these questions.

- Who are the main characters?
- Where and when does the series take place?
- Is the series funny, serious, exciting, or scary?

 **Tips** You can get ideas from:
- stories you have read.
- places you know.
- events in your life or someone else's life.

# 2 Think of a Story Idea

Create a brand new story for the series you have chosen. Imagine what might happen if:

- the characters go to a new place—a farm, the ocean, a city, outer space, or a park.

- a new character joins the series.

- the characters discover an unusual object, win a contest, or start a business.

Write down your ideas for a new episode. Choose the one you like best.

How Am I Doing?

**Before you begin to write your story outline, stop and ask yourself these questions:**

- **Is the episode about characters in a series?**

- **Do I know what will happen in the episode?**

## 3  Write a Story Outline

Now you have an idea for a new episode in your favorite series. Like all good stories, your episode should have a beginning, a middle, and an end. You can tell about the episode by writing a story outline. The outline doesn't have to be long. But it does need to give details about the story.

Here are some things you can include in your story outline:

- a list of the characters and a short description of each

- a couple of sentences telling where and when the episode takes place

- a short description of what happens in the episode

LASSIE:
My Story
By

Julian's Camping Trip
Place: The Beach
Time: Summer
Characters:
Julian
Huey, his
Glor

Julian's
Camping Trip

# 4 Present Your Story

Make an eye-catching cover for the story outline of your new episode. On it, write the series title, the episode's title, and your name.

Then, illustrate the cover with a scene from the story. Place your story outline in the classroom library. Read the story outlines written by your classmates. Did anyone write a new episode for the same series as you did? How are the episodes similar and different?

## If You Are Using a Computer ...

Make your episode's cover look really great! Experiment with different kinds and sizes of type for the title and your name. If you use the Sign format, you can place a decorative border around the title page.

BATMAN'S BIG ADVENTURE

by Keisha Thomas

**CONGRATULATIONS**

Now you have become a real hit-series author. Can you spot which new books, TV shows, and movies will become hit series?

Joanna Cole
and Bruce Degen
*Author and Illustrator* ▶

# Glossary

**a·do·be**
(ə dō′bē) *noun*
A sandy kind of clay used to make bricks. Sometimes bits of straw are mixed with the clay.

**cac·tus** (kak′təs) *noun*
A desert plant that has a thick stem covered with sharp spines instead of leaves.

**cam·ou·flaged**
(kam′ə fläzhd′)
*verb*
Disguised or hidden to avoid being easily seen.
▲ **camouflage**

cactus

**can·vas**
(kan′vəs) *noun*
A heavy, coarse cloth used for making tents, sails, and wagon covers.

**chased** (chāst) *verb*
Ran after and tried to catch. The dog *chased* the ball. ▲ **chase**

**chomp** (chomp) *verb*
Bite down on. Soon the rabbit will *chomp* on the carrot.

**com·pli·cat·ed**
(kom′pli kā′tid)
*adjective*
Not easy to understand or do. The boy couldn't understand the *complicated* directions for playing the game.

**coy·o·te** (kī ō′tē)
*noun*
An animal that looks like a small, thin wolf. It lives in North America and is closely related to wolves, foxes, and dogs.

**dem·on·strate**
(dem′ən strāt′) *verb*
Show or explain clearly. On Mondays, I often *demonstrate* how to use the computer.

coyote

desert

**des•ert** (dez′ərt) *noun*
A hot, dry, sandy land with little or no plant or animal life.

### Word Study

The word **desert** can be pronounced two ways. Each pronunciation has a different meaning. When you say dez′ərt, it means "a hot dry place." When you say di zûrt′, it means "to leave something behind; to abandon."

**de•tec•tive**
(di tek′tiv) *noun*
A person who follows clues to solve a crime.

**de•vour**
(di vour′) *verb*
Swallow or eat up eagerly. My hungry cats always *devour* their food.

**ex•hib•its**
(ig zib′its) *noun*
Groups of things that are shown. I saw four *exhibits* of old comic books at the book fair.
▲ **exhibit**

**field trip**
(fēld′ trip′) *noun*
A trip away from the classroom to learn about something. We took a *field trip* to the museum to study dinosaurs.

**ford** (fôrd) *noun*
A shallow place where a river can be crossed.

**fuz•zy** (fuz′ē) *adjective*
Covered with fine, loose fibers or hair. The stuffed bear was soft and *fuzzy*.

**gum•shoes**
(gum′shōōz′) *noun*
People who find clues and solve mysteries. The *gumshoes* solved three mysteries last month.
▲ **gumshoe**

### Word Study

The words *gum* and *shoe* were originally put together to describe *shoe* with *gum*—or rubber—soles. Then **gumshoe** became a slang word for a detective or private eye who goes around quietly on *gum* soled *shoes*.

| | | | | | |
|---|---|---|---|---|---|
| a | add | ŏŏ | took | ə = | |
| ā | ace | ōō | pool | a in *above* | |
| â | care | u | up | e in *sicken* | |
| ä | palm | û | burn | i in *possible* | |
| e | end | yōō | fuse | o in *melon* | |
| ē | equal | oi | oil | u in *circus* | |
| i | it | ou | pout | | |
| ī | ice | ng | ring | | |
| o | odd | th | thin | | |
| ō | open | th | this | | |
| ô | order | zh | vision | | |

# Glossary

**hab·i·tat** (hab′i tat′) *noun*
The place where an animal or plant naturally lives and grows. A whale's *habitat* is the ocean.

**hitched** (hicht) *verb*
Tied or fastened with a rope. She *hitched* the mule to the wagon.
▲ **hitch**

javelina

**ja·ve·li·na** (hä′və lē′nə) *noun*
A wild pig that lives in the southwestern United States and Mexico; a peccary.

**land·scape** (land′skāp′) *noun*
A view or scene of surrounding land. The *landscape* was filled with trees and mountains.

**lurched** (lûrcht) *verb*
Suddenly swayed in one direction or from side to side. The car *lurched* forward and then came to a stop. ▲ **lurch**

**par·tic·i·pants** (pär tis′ə pənts) *noun*
People who join others in an activity. All the *participants* in the parade wore funny costumes.
▲ **participant**

**poi·son·ous** (poi′zə nəs) *adjective*
Having a harmful substance that can harm or kill. The bite of a *poisonous* spider can make you very sick.

**pray·ing man·tis** (prā′ing man′tis) *noun*
An insect with long sticklike legs and a triangle-shaped head. It is related to the grasshopper.

**proj·ect** (proj′ekt) *noun*
A special study, task, or activity. I collected sea shells for my science *project*.

**run·ning gear** (run′ing gēr′) *noun*
The part of a wagon that the wheels and steering bar are connected to.

**solve** (solv) *verb*
To find the answer to a problem or mystery. The detectives will *solve* the crime and catch the criminal.

**speck·led** (spek′əld) *adjective*
Covered with small dots of different colors. We saw a brown-and-white *speckled* hen.

**splash** (splash) *verb*
To hit or move through water so that it is thrown about.

praying mantis

**stalk·ing** (stô′king) *verb*
Following someone or something so as to get close without being seen. The cat was *stalking* a large black beetle.
▲ **stalk**

**ta·ble** (tā′bəl) *noun*
A piece of furniture with a flat top. It is held up by one or more legs.

### Word History

The word **table** comes from a Latin word that means "a board." Long ago, people placed things on boards, just as we put things on *tables* today.

**track** (trak) *verb*
To follow the footprints or trail of something or someone. The rangers will *track* the bear to its den.

**trail** (trāl) *noun*
The series of marks or clues left behind by a person or animal. We followed the *trail* of the deer into the forest.

**tum·ble·weeds**
(tum′bəl wedz′) *noun*
Bushy plants that grow in the deserts and plains of western North America. In the autumn, the wind breaks *tumbleweeds* off at their roots and blows them around. ▲ **tumbleweed**

**wee·vil** (wē′vəl) *noun*
A kind of beetle that feeds on cotton, fruits, and grain. A weevil is usually thought to be a pest by farmers.

| | | | | | |
|---|---|---|---|---|---|
| a | add | o͝o | took | ə = | |
| ā | ace | o͞o | pool | | a in *above* |
| â | care | u | up | | e in *sicken* |
| ä | palm | û | burn | | i in *possible* |
| e | end | yo͞o | fuse | | o in *melon* |
| ē | equal | oi | oil | | u in *circus* |
| i | it | ou | pout | | |
| ī | ice | ng | ring | | |
| o | odd | th | thin | | |
| ō | open | th | this | | |
| ô | order | zh | vision | | |

**tumbleweeds**

# Authors & Illustrators

### Jim Harris *pages 108–120*

When this Southwestern artist looks out of his studio window, he sometimes sees elk and other wildlife walking by. And every night he hears the coyotes howl! In the story of *The Three Little Javelinas*, the character named Coyote was inspired by the tales of the Tohono O'Odham tribe. In their traditional stories, Coyote is a trickster who is always getting outsmarted by others!

### Ann M. Martin *pages 34–47*

This best-selling author says that she writes her books to entertain herself as well as the young people who read them. When Martin writes a story, she is often reliving memories from her own childhood. When she was young, her parents encouraged her to help others. This attitude is still very important to Ann Martin, and that's one reason why the girls in the Baby-sitters Club are always so active in their community.

### Jean Marzollo   *pages 62–65*

This author enjoys working on the *I Spy* series because these books are "beautiful and fun at the same time." Walter Wick takes the pictures first, and then Jean Marzollo lets the pictures inspire her to come up with her rhyming riddles. This author has also written rhymes for other books, including the nonfiction books *In 1776* and *In 1492*.

### Donald J. Sobol   *pages 68–76*

Over 30 years ago, Donald J. Sobol decided to write a mystery book for kids. That book was called *Encyclopedia Brown, Boy Detective*. Sobol wrote the whole book in just two weeks! Since then, he has completed many more books about everyone's favorite boy detective. He's proud that his books offer both challenging mysteries and lots of laughs. Sobol says this about his famous boy detective, "Encyclopedia is the kid I wanted to be when I was ten years old!"

### Laura Ingalls Wilder   *pages 90–103*

In 1930, a 63-year-old farm woman sat down at her kitchen table to write about her pioneer childhood. That woman was Laura Ingalls Wilder, and her story grew into a series called The Little House books. To Wilder's great surprise, her books became famous. Children all over the world read her stories and kept asking for more. Wilder wrote eight books in all. Laura Ingalls Wilder died in 1957 at the age of 90, but her story lives on in her popular series.

**"I lived everything that happened in my books. It is a long story, filled with sunshine and shadow...."**

# Books &

## Author Study

**More by Joanna Cole**

**Bully Trouble**
Big Eddie is a bully who is always picking on Arlo and Robby. What can these two friends do to make Eddie stop being a bully?

**Scholastic's The Magic School Bus® at the Waterworks**
Ride along with Ms. Frizzle and her class as they explore the inner workings of the local waterworks. Laugh at Bruce Degen's great illustrations.

## Fiction

**Commander Toad in Space**
*by Jane Yolen*
*illustrated by Bruce Degen*
Brave and Bright. Bright and Brave. Commander Toad and the crew of *Star Warts* travel through space in this science-fiction series.

**Henry and Beezus**
*by Beverly Cleary*
Before she wrote about Ramona, Beverly Cleary wrote funny books about Ramona's neighbor, Henry Huggins. In this book, Henry and Beezus become friends when she helps him raise money to buy a new bike.

**Julian's Glorious Summer**
*by Ann Cameron*
Julian is the kind of boy who easily finds adventure. In this book, Julian finds lots to do during his summer vacation.

## Nonfiction

**George Washington Carver: The Peanut Scientist**
*by Patricia and Fredrick McKissack*
What's so special about a peanut? Find out when you read the life story of this great African-American scientist.

**... If You Lived in Colonial Times**
*by Ann McGovern*
What did people in colonial times wear? This book, and the others in this series, use questions and answers to explain what life was like long ago.

**Picture Book of Helen Keller**
*by David Adler*
*illustrated by John and Alexandra Wallner*
Helen Keller was blind and deaf. With the help of a special teacher, Helen learned to read and write.

# xMedia

## Videos

### Lassie, Come Home
*MGM/UA Home Video*
Lassie, the popular dog star, first appeared in this movie. In it, the brave collie journeys hundreds of miles to rejoin the family she loves.
(93 minutes)

### Kristy and the Great Campaign
*(Baby-sitters Club Videos)*
*Scholastic Inc./Good Times*
In this film, based on the hit series, Kristy decides to help Courtney campaign for president of the third grade.
(30 minutes)

### Newton's Apple
*Pacific Arts*
This award-winning television series makes science fun. Experts answer questions kids have asked about all kinds of topics.
(60 minutes)

## Software

### Arthur's Teacher Trouble
*(Living Book Series)*
*Broderbund*
*(Macintosh, CD-ROM)*
Arthur the Aardvark is the star of a series of books by Marc Brown. Now you can use this interactive program to join in Arthur's adventures as he prepares for a big spelling bee. This software also lets you choose the language you want to use— English or Spanish.

### Super Story Tree
*Scholastic Inc. (Apple, IBM)*
Write a story, draw pictures, even add music and sound effects! Here's a program that will help you to write and draw a sequel to an existing series, or create a new series of your own.

## Magazines

### Spider
*Open Court Publishing*
This popular magazine contains stories, poems, and articles on all kinds of subjects. It gets its name from a cartoon spider that appears throughout each issue.

### DuckTales Magazine
*Welsh Publishing Group*
Scrooge McDuck and his three nephews star in their own TV series— and in this magazine. This entertainment magazine for kids includes lots of funny stories, comic strips, and puzzles.

## A Place to Write

One of Laura Ingalls Wilder's "little houses" is now a museum. For more information about the author and her times, write to:

**Laura Ingalls Wilder**
**Home and Museum**
**Rocky Ridge Farm**
**Mansfield, MO 65704**

# Acknowledgments

Grateful acknowledgment is made to the following sources for permission to reprint from previously published material. The publisher has made diligent efforts to trace the ownership of all copyrighted material in this volume and believes that all necessary permissions have been secured. If any errors or omissions have inadvertently been made, proper corrections will gladly be made in future editions.

**Cover:** BABAR: Illustration from THE STORY OF BABAR by Jean de Brunhoff. Copyright © 1933 and renewed 1961 by Random House, Inc. Reprinted by permission of Random House, Inc. BATMAN: Batman image property of DC Comics. Used by permission. Batman is a trademark of DC Comics copyright © 1992. All rights reserved. CLIFFORD: Clifford® by Norman Bridwell from CLIFFORD GETS A JOB by Norman Bridwell. Copyright © 1965 by Norman Bridwell. Reprinted by permission. CLIFFORD is a registered trademark of Norman Bridwell. JULIAN: Cover illustration from MORE STORIES JULIAN TELLS by Ann Cameron, illustrated by Ann Strugnell. Illustration copyright © 1986 by Ann Strugnell. Reprinted by permission of Alfred A. Knopf, Inc. KERMIT: Kermit the Frog is copyrighted and used by special permission of Jim Henson Productions. LASSIE: Photograph by Daniel R. Westergren © National Geographic Society. Used by permission. MS. FRIZZLE: Illustration by Bruce Degen. Illustration copyright © 1994 by Bruce Degen. Reprinted by permission. THE MAGIC SCHOOL BUS is a registered trademark of Scholastic Inc.

**Interior:** PETER RABBIT: Illustration from THE TALE OF PETER RABBIT by Beatrix Potter. Copyright © 1902, 1987 by Frederick Warne & Co. Used by permission. BOXCAR CHILDREN: Cover illustration from THE MYSTERY OF THE HIDDEN PAINTING by Gertrude Chandler Warner. Cover illustration copyright © 1993 by Scholastic Inc. Reprinted by permission. THE BOXCAR CHILDREN is a registered trademark of Albert Whitman & Company. MADELINE: Illustration from MADELINE AND THE GYPSIES by Ludwig Bemelmans. Copyright © 1958, 1959 by Ludwig Bemelmans, renewed copyright © 1986, 1987 by Madeleine Bemelmans and Barbara Bemelmans. Used by permission of Viking Penguin, a division of Penguin Books USA Inc. BATMAN: Batman image property of DC Comics. Used by permission. Batman is a trademark of DC Comics copyright © 1992. All rights reserved. LASSIE: Photograph by Daniel R. Westergren © National Geographic Society. Used by permission. RAMONA: Illustration from RAMONA QUIMBY, AGE 8 by Beverly Cleary, illustrated by Alan Tiegreen. Copyright © 1981 by Beverly Cleary. Used by permission of Morrow Junior Books, a division of William Morrow & Company, Inc. CHARLIE BROWN: © 1950 United Feature Syndicate, Inc. Used by permission. SNOOPY: © 1958 United Feature Syndicate, Inc. Used by permission. BABAR: Illustration from THE STORY OF BABAR by Jean de Brunhoff. Copyright © 1933, renewed 1961 by Random House, Inc. Reprinted by permission of Random House, Inc. CLIFFORD: Illustration from CLIFFORD GETS A JOB by Norman Bridwell. Copyright © 1965 by Norman Bridwell. Reprinted by permission. CLIFFORD is a registered trademark of Norman Bridwell. ENCYCLOPEDIA BROWN:

Illustration from ENCYCLOPEDIA BROWN, BOY DETECTIVE by Donald J. Sobol. Copyright © 1963 by Donald J. Sobol. Used by permission of Lodestar Books, an affiliate of Dutton Children's Books, a division of Penguin USA Inc. KERMIT: Kermit the Frog is copyrighted and used by special permission of Jim Henson Productions. CHAPULIN COLORADO: Chapulin Colorado used by permission of Televisa, Mexico. AMELIA BEDELIA: character image from one illustration from PLAY BALL, AMELIA BEDELIA by Peggy Parish, illustration by Wallace Tripp. Illustrations copyright © 1972 by Wallace Tripp. Reprinted by permission of HarperCollins Publishers. JULIAN: Cover illustration from MORE STORIES JULIAN TELLS by Ann Cameron, illustrated by Ann Strugnell. Illustration copyright © 1986 by Ann Strugnell. Reprinted by permission of Alfred A. Knopf, Inc. CARMEN SANDIEGO: Where in the World is Carmen Sandiego?® is based on the computer games from Brøderbund Software, Inc. Where in the World is Carmen Sandiego?®, Carmen Sandiego™ and the logo design are trademarks of Brøderbund Software, Inc. Used with permission. IKTOMI: Illustration from IKTOMI AND THE BERRIES by Paul Goble. Copyright © 1989 by Paul Goble. Used by permission of Orchard Books, New York. TIME WARP TRIO: Illustration from YOUR MOTHER WAS A NEANDERTHAL by Jon Scieszka, illustrated by Lane Smith. Illustration copyright © 1993 by Lane Smith. Used by permission of Viking Penguin, a division of Penguin Books USA Inc. MS. FRIZZLE: Illustration from THE MAGIC SCHOOL BUS LOST IN THE SOLAR SYSTEM by Joanna Cole, illustrated by Bruce Degen. Illustration copyright © 1990 by Bruce Degen. Reprinted by permission of Scholastic Inc. THE MAGIC SCHOOL BUS is a registered trademark of Scholastic Inc. BABY-SITTERS CLUB: Cover illustration from THE BABY-SITTERS REMEMBER by Ann M. Martin. Cover illustration copyright © 1994 by Scholastic Inc. THE BABY-SITTERS CLUB is a registered trademark of Scholastic Inc. Reprinted by permission. "The Magic School Bus Hops Home" is an adaptation of a production script by Jocelyn Stevenson based on THE MAGIC SCHOOL BUS book series by Joanna Cole and Bruce Degen. Copyright © 1995 by Joanna Cole and Bruce Degen. All rights reserved. Used by permission. Major funding for Scholastic's THE MAGIC SCHOOL BUS television project is provided by Microsoft Home, makers of a broad line of quality software for your home computer. Additional funding is provided by U.S. Department of Energy and Carnegie Corporation of New York. Presented on PBS by SCETV. Book covers from THE MAGIC SCHOOL BUS series: THE MSB ON THE OCEAN FLOOR illustration copyright © 1992 by Bruce Degen. THE MSB LOST IN THE SOLAR SYSTEM illustration copyright © 1990 by Bruce Degen. THE MSB INSIDE THE HUMAN BODY illustration copyright © 1989 by Bruce Degen. THE MSB INSIDE THE EARTH illustration copyright © 1987 by Bruce Degen. THE MSB IN THE TIME OF THE DINOSAURS illustration copyright © 1994 by Bruce Degen. Reprinted by permission of Scholastic Inc. THE MAGIC SCHOOL BUS is a registered trademark of Scholastic Inc.

Illustrations of Ms. Frizzle (pp. 30-33) from THE MAGIC SCHOOL BUS LOST IN THE SOLAR SYSTEM by Joanna Cole, illustrated by Bruce Degen. Illustration copyright © 1990 by Bruce Degen. Reprinted by permission of Scholastic Inc.

Excerpt, cover, and logo from THE BABY-SITTERS CLUB #36: JESSI'S BABY-SITTER by Ann M. Martin, cover art by Hodges Soileau. Text copyright © 1990 by Ann M. Martin. Cover illustration © 1988 by Scholastic Inc. Book covers from THE BABY-SITTERS CLUB series: KRISTY'S GREAT IDEA cover illustration copyright © 1986 by Scholastic Inc. HELLO MALLORY cover illustration by Hodges Soileau. Illustration copyright © 1990 by Scholastic Inc. Reprinted by permission of Scholastic Inc. THE BABY-SITTERS CLUB and APPLE PAPERBACKS are registered trademarks of Scholastic Inc.

Selections and cover from INCREDIBLE MINI-BEASTS by Christopher Maynard. Photography by Frank Greenaway, Neil Fletcher, Jane Burton, Kim Taylor, Stephen Oliver and Colin Keates. Copyright © 1994 by Covent Garden Books Ltd. Book covers from INCREDIBLE LITTLE MONSTERS, INCREDIBLE FLYING MACHINES, and INCREDIBLE DINOSAURS, all by Christopher Maynard, copyright © 1994 by Covent Garden Books Ltd. Used by permission of Snapshot™, an imprint of Covent Garden Books and Elan Press (UK).

Selections and covers from I SPY: A BOOK OF PICTURE RIDDLES and I SPY FANTASY: A BOOK OF PICTURE RIDDLES. Photographs by Walter Wick, riddles by Jean Marzollo. I SPY: A BOOK OF PICTURE RIDDLES text copyright © 1992 by Jean Marzollo. Illustrations and photographs copyright © 1992 by Walter Wick. I SPY FANTASY text copyright © 1994 by Jean Marzollo. Illustrations and photographs copyright © 1994 by Walter Wick. Book cover from I SPY CHRISTMAS, illustrations and photographs copyright © 1992 by Walter Wick. Book covers from I SPY MYSTERY and I SPY FUNHOUSE, photographs copyright © 1993 by Walter Wick. Reprinted by permission of Scholastic Inc. I SPY is a registered trademark of Scholastic Inc.

"The Case of the Runaway Elephant" and cover from ENCYCLOPEDIA BROWN LENDS A HAND by Donald J. Sobol, illustrated by Leonard Shortall. Text copyright © 1974 by Donald J. Sobol. Illustrations copyright © 1974 by Thomas Nelson, Inc. Used by permission of Lodestar Books, an affiliate of Dutton Children's Books, a division of Penguin USA Inc. Illustrations on pp. 68, 73, and 76 by Leonard Shortall from ENCYCLOPEDIA BROWN, BOY DETECTIVE by Donald J. Sobol. Copyright © 1963 by Donald J. Sobol. Book covers from ENCYCLOPEDIA BROWN, BOY DETECTIVE and ENCYCLOPEDIA BROWN TRACKS THEM DOWN, cover illustrations copyright © 1982 by Dick Williams. Used by permission of Lodestar Books, an affiliate of Dutton Children's Books, a division of Penguin USA Inc. Book covers from ENCYCLOPEDIA BROWN KEEPS THE PEACE and ENCYCLOPEDIA BROWN GETS HIS MAN, cover illustrations copyright © 1982 by Dick Williams. Reprinted by permission of Bantam Books, a division of Bantam Doubleday Dell Publishing Group, Inc. Book covers from ENCYCLOPEDIA BROWN CARRIES ON and ENCYCLOPEDIA BROWN SETS THE PACE, cover illustrations copyright © 1982 by Scholastic Inc. APPLE PAPERBACKS is a registered trademark of Scholastic Inc.

Selections and cover from 101 ELEPHANT JOKES compiled by Robert Blake. Copyright © 1964 by Scholastic Inc. Used by permission.

Illustrations and logo of Carmen Sandiego are used by permission of Brøderbund. Where in the World is Carmen Sandiego?® is based on the computer games from Brøderbund Software, Inc. Where in the